Ballymaloe

Bread Book

Tim Allen

Gill & Macmillan

Gill & Macmillan Ltd
Hume Avenue
Park West
Dublin 12
with associated companies throughout the world
www.gillmacmillan.ie

0 7171 2931 4

Index compiled by Susan Williams
Design by Slick Fish Design, Dublin
Print origination by Carole Lynch
Printed by GraphyCems, Spain

*The paper used in this book is made from the wood pulp of
managed forests. For every tree felled, at least one tree
is planted, thereby renewing natural resources.*

A catalogue record is available for this book
from the British Library.

5 4 3

For
My wife Darina,
The original simply delicious

Contents

Contents

Acknowledgments

I would like to thank my daughters-in-law Rachel and Penny for helping me in testing the recipes for this book. Also a big thank you to all the staff of the cookery school for their enthusiasm and interest, and for enabling me to take the time I needed to research and test recipes and write this book.

A very special word of thanks to my friend and PA Margot Heskin. I can honestly say if it wasn't for her dedication and staying power this book would never have been finished. I am indebted to her for her understanding of an editorial brief, for organising and planning my work schedule and keeping me to the grindstone.

For my mother Myrtle Allen of Ballymaloe House, for her interest and encouragement and for introducing to us as children the most delicious of all brown breads.

My daughters Lydia and Emily who cheerfully interrupted me, often with my excited grandson Joshua in tow. Their encouragement and chatter was always welcome.

A debt of gratitude that cannot be properly expressed is owed to my wife Darina for her vision; without her we would not have a cookery school and I may never have had the opportunity both to make and teach these breads. Her extraordinary knowledge and understanding of all things culinary never ceases to astonish me.

The father and daughter team of Kevin and Sally Dunne whose photographs rock.

And last but not least my publisher Michael Gill for believing that there was a book there.

Introduction to the Ballymaloe Bread Book

As I sit here writing the introduction to this, my first book, it is hard to recall exactly how I became so passionate about bread and so fascinated by it.

My friends don't seem to be too surprised that I have written this book but, I have to admit, I am. I had never seen myself as a writer, and when the idea was first suggested to me I was stunned and mildly amused. My wife Darina had always been the one who wrote cookery books, not me.

Time passed. Not only were my friends encouraging me to share my knowledge but my wife and children were too; then students past and present expressed an eagerness to have a bread recipe book written by me.

Since 1968, I had been running our home, Kinoith, as a farm, growing lettuces, mushrooms, tomatoes and apples and other crops, but by the early 1980s it had become uneconomical to continue. Prices for my produce were dropping. Farming in Ireland had become increasingly difficult and the type of growing and farming I was involved in was no longer viable. We had to diversify, find new ways to use our land.

We had four children aged between two and twelve. Darina had been giving cookery lessons at my parents' country house hotel, Ballymaloe House, with my mother, Myrtle

Allen, for a number of years and we felt there was an opening for a cookery school. A cookery school that would both celebrate and teach the wonders of Irish food and ingredients, a philosophy that my parents had promoted since they started Ballymaloe House. Darina had spent a week with Marcella Hazzan in Italy at her cookery school and returned fired with enthusiasm and ideas. We decided that there was such a wealth of wonderful fish, meat, vegetables, fruit and so on in Ireland that we could teach people how to value and use what we had. And finally put an end to the myth that as a nation we live solely on boiled bacon, cabbage and potatoes!

So in 1983 I swapped roles with Darina. She concentrated on establishing our new cookery school and I looked after the children. To us, our role-reversal seemed a perfectly natural thing to do. And as the children grew older I began to take a more active role in both the running of the school and as a teacher. Darina and I now work side by side.

The Ballymaloe Cookery School attracts students from all over the world. We run two professional courses a year and many more short courses for the interested amateur.

For me, my awareness of bread-making go right back to when I was a tiny child of about two. I remember being able to just peer over the top of the work counter in the kitchen of my childhood home in Ballymaloe. I could see the tea-towels draped mysteriously over the dome of the bread tin. No mystery now — of course, this was brown yeast bread rising by the warmth of the Aga.

Bread-making was part of our daily lives then; there was always bread rising or baking somewhere. But my real treat as a young boy was the delivery that came once or twice a week from Daly's bakery in Cloyne. I recall vividly those most delicious of white yeast loaves. We cut them thickly and fought over the heel, that greatly prized slice — spread with butter and strawberry jam. It was a special bread I will never forget. It was not until Mrs Wall closed her bakery that we began to make our own white yeast bread at home.

Now the best loaf of white yeast bread is made by Mary Cusack in Ballymaloe. She bakes these loaves every morning for the guests staying in Ballymaloe. She has been making white yeast bread since she was just fifteen or sixteen years old. To me, her bread comes as close to perfection in a loaf of white bread as you can come.

I didn't start to make bread myself until I was married with a family. One weekend I found myself with my young son Isaac stranded in Kinoith without a car. I decided to make some bread. I knew the method instinctively as I had often been asked as a young boy to keep an eye on the bread as it rose and to tell my mother when it was ready for baking. And I knew I had all the ingredients I needed to make that loaf. But I was stuck on the exact quantities. I phoned my mother. She gave me the recipe and it worked beautifully. I was thrilled.

From then on, I baked brown and white soda bread for my children as they grew up. I have a clear memory of the first year we took a boat on the Shannon with the children. I hadn't thought about bringing ingredients to make any bread, but quickly realised I needed to make a loaf as my children would only eat 'Daddy's Bread'. Nothing else would do. I stopped off in a shop and had to ask the shopkeeper to divide the flour into 1 lb bags as I had no weighing scales on the boat. In future when we travelled on the Shannon I always remembered to take what I needed and weighed my flour before I left home!

When my youngest child, Emily, went to school I began to work full-time in the Ballymaloe Cookery School and it was then that I started to bake yeast bread again.

I was fascinated as a teacher to see how some people had no difficulty in mastering the technique of making a loaf of bread, but others seemed to find it very hard. So, after realising how the students struggled with something that was a natural part of my life, I decided to really look at how I could best teach people to make bread. I was intrigued — and hooked.

I quickly saw that many people have a mental block when it comes to yeast bread in particular. They think it must take a lot of time to make a loaf. But in reality the bread does not demand a lot of your time. It is quite happy to rise alone in the warmth. The initial mixing and kneading takes only about 10 minutes. And after that the bread will only demand your attention for a further 10 minutes. Just don't neglect it completely!

The difficulty people have with soda bread is the temptation to over-mix it. They just can't quite accept that it only needs the gentlest of mixing, then into the oven. No kneading at all.

Bread is, after all, just flour, water, leavening — and you. You mix it, then leave it to ferment and grow. It is alive. Just like any other food source that has the fermentation process in its production. Take cheese, which is just milk; the end result depends on how the cheese-maker treats the milk. Wine is another example; it is just grapes, wild yeast and the wine-maker.

So what is it about bread that is mystical? What is it that holds you in its grip? Is it the never-ending pursuit of the perfect loaf?

I know the anticipation I feel never lessens as I wait to taste a piece of every new batch.

I felt the same sense of excitement when I used to develop my own photographs — the anticipation as I waited in the darkroom to view my negatives would grow as I opened my developing tank, unspooled my film and held it up to the light — such a thrill. No two rolls were ever the same.

And no two loaves are ever the same.

Nothing seems to give more pleasure then taking that first loaf of bread from the oven. There is a sense of pride mixed with astonishment. As a teacher, I get such pleasure watching a student lift out their first loaf of bread. The look on their face, the joy and amazement that lights up their eyes, can't easily be described.

Often students chase around the school looking for me when their bread is out of the oven, such is their excitement. It doesn't matter if I am in a meeting or working at my desk, I will be found. They are determined to share their triumph and show me the bread they have made. These are not children, my students are adults, but the joy they feel about their first loaf of bread is certainly a childlike and genuine one.

So here I am, my book written. My hope is that when you read this book you will start to make bread for yourself. For some, bread-making will be a new skill; for others, a long-

forgotten pleasure. Or the book may revive childhood memories of a beloved mother or grandmother. Though all our lives seem so much busier, faster and more demanding these days, perhaps, by letting me be your guide on this fascinating journey, you can recapture that most basic and simple of pleasures. Stop a while and take time to rediscover the wonderful process of making bread; it is something that used to take place daily in almost every home in the land.

When you make bread it is such a pleasing process, a fulfilling combination of the aroma of freshly baked bread, pride in your finished loaf and the delight you feel in seeing others enjoy something you have created. And the sense of relaxation that bread-making can provide is fantastic. Kneading the white yeast dough, from a shaggy, uneven ball to a smooth living dough in your hands is both sensuous and satisfying.

To me, walking into a house that smells of freshly baked bread is the ultimate welcome.

The basics when making your own bread are quite simple. You need to measure accurately, and use the best quality ingredients you can. Knead and let the dough rise for just the right length of time. Get to know your oven; it will no doubt have its own personality and you will, in time, become familiar with its temperatures and times. Explore your kitchen, find the warmest spots to rise your bread. Discover the work surface that is the right height for you to knead on, and that provides you with enough space to work.

Don't neglect your tools. Finding the right equipment is also important. The mixer you use, the bowls, the bread tins, the dough scraper, the weighing scales. All of these are important in the creation of your bread. Over time you will find the ways of working that suit you best.

Read the recipes carefully before you start. Check you have the ingredients you need close by. Preheat your oven, lay out the equipment you may require. This way you will be able to work smoothly and easily. Carelessness and over-baking are equally bad traits for a baker to have.

The more often you make a bread the more you will become used to it. The first time it will be daunting, the second less so, third even less, and so on.

Don't be afraid of making mistakes. They are how you will learn, use them as your guide. Some of the best bread may start from a mistake.

The more you bake, the more confident you will become. Then you can start to experiment with new flavours and textures. You can add spices, nuts, dried fruits to your favourite recipes and create your own unique loaf.

Bread-making is part artistic and part scientific, and it also involves a good deal of practice and familiarity. To me, making bread is a natural part of who I am. I don't even have to think about it.

Welcome to a new world.

Note to the

Recipes

As some of the bread recipes given in each section of the book form the basis for so many interesting and delicious variations, and to avoid excessive repetition, some recipes include cross-references back to the basic recipes or to other parts of the book. With practice, I hope that you will become so familiar with all the steps involved in making

each basic bread that, in time, you will hardly need to turn the page!

I have also provided a useful glossary at the back of the book to help you with some of the cookery terms used and to give you extra tips and reminders.

Introduction to
Soda Bread

Soda bread is indigenous to Ireland and our climate. It reflects the soft, gentle nature of the people and the weather. It was first made in the early nineteenth century when bread soda, also known as bicarbonate of soda or baking soda, became widely available. With the discovery of the combination of our soft, flaky, wholemeal flour with readily available sour milk, it became a staple in every Irish family. It was originally cooked as a griddle bread over an open fire and served with country butter.

In some parts of Ireland soda bread is called soda cake. It has continued to be made up to the present day in many Irish homes where sour milk has been replaced by cultured buttermilk that can be bought in most local shops around the country. However, you can also make your own buttermilk by starting a buttermilk plant at home. Full details are given on page 139.

I often say the skill in making a soda bread well is actually more of an art than a science. It's in your hands and the way you handle the flour and the dough.

It is a wonderfully quick bread to make. Whether we are going on a boating holiday on the Shannon or taking a house in West Cork, before we leave we weigh up bags for white soda bread, brown soda bread and Spotted Dog. So at a moment's notice when the troops descend we can have fresh bread in under an hour. We call this our pre-weighed repertoire!

There are many variations on the basic recipe for soda bread. As you will see, you can be very adventurous and creative with the flavourings you add, though I am not sure our ancestors would recognise the Rosemary and Sun-dried Tomato Soda Bread (see page 3), let alone our Stripy Cat on page 6. Stripy Cat is a chocolate version of the traditional Spotted Dog (see page 4). You could say this is an Irish version of the French *pain au chocolat*!

There are a few crucial watch points when making soda bread to ensure a light yummy loaf:

- Make sure you fully preheat the oven.
- Choose a large enough bowl, at least 25.5 cm/10 in wide, in fact a plastic washing-up bowl is ideal.
- Make sure you always measure all the ingredients carefully.
- Finely sieve the bread soda as the lumps do not dissolve in the liquid.
- Be careful not to over-mix the dough, just mix it until it comes together.
- With floured hands roll the dough gently on the work surface.
- Place your dough on the baking tray before cutting the cross in it.
- *Have fun!*
- Time is a guide.

White Soda Bread

Whoever would have thought that white flour, buttermilk, salt and a little raising agent could produce such a delicious bread? So quick and easy, it's a must for everyone to learn. There is no faster bread. This tasty recipe is the basis for a whole range of flavoured breads and also makes a superb quick base for pizza and focaccia (see page 65).

Makes:	1 loaf
Cooking time:	35 minutes, approximately
What you need:	• 450 g/1 lb plain white flour, preferably unbleached
	• 1 level teaspoon salt
	• 1 level teaspoon bread soda, finely sieved
	• 400 ml/14 fl oz buttermilk, approximately
What you do:	First, fully preheat the oven to 230°C/450°F/regulo 8.

Sieve the flour, salt and bread soda into a large, wide mixing bowl.

Make a well in the centre. Pour most of the milk into the flour. Using one hand with the fingers open and stiff, mix in a full circle drawing in the flour from the sides of the bowl, adding more milk if necessary. The dough should be softish, not too wet and sticky.

The trick with all soda breads is not to over-mix the dough. Mix the dough as quickly and as gently as possible, keeping it really light and airy. When the dough all comes together, turn it out onto a well-floured work surface. Wash and dry your hands.

Gently roll the ball of dough around with floury hands for a few seconds, just enough to tidy it up. Then pat it gently into a round, about 5 cm/2 in high.

Place the dough on a lightly floured baking sheet. With a sharp knife cut a deep cross in it, letting the cuts go over the sides of the bread. Then prick the four triangles with your knife: according to Irish folklore this will let the fairies out!

Put this into your preheated oven for 10 minutes, then turn the heat down to 200°C/400°F/regulo 6 for a further 25 minutes, or until cooked. When the bread is cooked it will sound hollow when tapped.

White Soda Bread with Herbs

This is a delicious variation on the traditional white soda bread. The combination of freshly chopped herbs brings an unusual sweetness to the bread. I often serve it with home-made soup.

Makes:	1 loaf
Cooking time:	35 minutes, approximately
What you need:	• 450 g/1 lb plain white flour, preferably unbleached • 1 level teaspoon salt • 1 level teaspoon bread soda, finely sieved • 1 dessertspoon each of rosemary, sage and chives, all freshly chopped • 400 ml/14 fl oz buttermilk, approximately
What you do:	First fully preheat the oven to 230°C/450°F/regulo 8. Sieve the flour, salt and bread soda into a large, wide mixing bowl. Add the freshly chopped herbs to the dry ingredients. Once you have got this far, follow the rest of the steps exactly as described for White Soda Bread on page 2. Don't forget to prick the triangles of dough to let the fairies out before you bake the bread.

White Soda Bread with Rosemary and Sun-dried Tomatoes

Whoever said soda bread had to be plain? Inspired by the increase in flavoured breads available in supermarkets and good food shops these days, I have found the traditional Irish Soda Bread is very easy to adapt to new ideas. There are few breads that can be prepared and out of the oven in just 40 minutes.

Makes: 1 loaf

Cooking time: 35 minutes, approximately

What you need:
- 450 g/1 lb plain white flour, preferably unbleached
- 1 level teaspoon salt
- 1 level teaspoon bread soda, finely sieved
- 1 level tablespoons of chopped rosemary
- 2 tablespoons of chopped sun-dried tomatoes
- 400 ml/14 fl oz buttermilk, approximately

What you do: First, fully preheat the oven to 230°C/450°F/regulo 8.

Sieve the flour, salt and bread soda into a large, wide mixing bowl. Gently mix the chopped rosemary and sun-dried tomatoes into the dry ingredients.

Now from here, you can prepare the mixture and bake this tasty bread by following the instructions given in the basic White Soda Bread recipe on page 2.

Spotted Dog

Spotted Dog is also called Railway Cake in some parts of the country — 'a currant for every station' as the saying goes! In my case, it would be 'a sultana for every station' as I prefer these for their more luscious flavour. This bread is one of the great homely foods of our family. It has always been a favourite with my children, freshly made on a Sunday morning for our picnics on the cliffs at Ballyandreen, or relished with lashings of butter, jam and steaming mugs of drinking chocolate after a winter walk on Shanagarry strand.

It was also a staple in our pre-weighed repertoire made on our family boating trips on the Shannon and given as a parting gift to the many boating friends we made on the way.

Makes: 1 loaf

Cooking time: 45 minutes, approximately

What you need:
- 450 g/1 lb plain white flour, preferably unbleached
- 1 level teaspoon salt
- 1 level teaspoon bread soda, finely sieved
- 1 dessertspoon sugar
- 85–110 g/3–4 oz sultanas
- 350 ml/12 fl oz buttermilk, approximately
- 1 egg

What you do:
First, fully preheat your oven to 220°C/425°F/regulo 7.

Into a large mixing bowl, sieve the flour and bread soda, and then add the salt, sugar and fruit. Mix the ingredients well together by lifting them up above the bowl and letting them fall loosely back into the bowl through your fingers. This adds more air and therefore more lightness to your finished bread.

Now make a well in the centre of the flour. Break the egg into the bottom of your measuring jug and add the buttermilk up to the 400 ml/14 fl oz level, so that the egg makes up part of your total liquid measurement. Pour most of this milk and egg mixture into the flour.

Using your hand as usual when making any soda bread, with the fingers open and stiff, mix in a full circle drawing in the flour from the sides of the bowl, adding more milk and egg mixture if necessary. The dough should be nice and soft, but not too wet and sticky.

With Spotted Dog, as with all soda breads, you must avoid over-mixing the dough. Mix as quickly and as gently as possible to keep the dough light and airy. When the dough all comes together, turn it out onto a well-floured work surface. Wash and dry your hands.

As with our previous soda bread recipes, with floured fingers roll lightly for a few seconds, just enough to tidy it up. Then pat the dough into a round, pressing to about 6 cm/2 in high.

Place the dough on a baking tray dusted lightly with flour. Cut a deep cross in it and prick each of the dough triangles with your knife.

Put the dough into the preheated oven for 10 minutes, then turn the heat down to 200°C/400°F/regulo 6 and cook for a further 35 minutes, or until cooked. If you are in doubt about the bread being cooked, tap the bottom. If it is cooked it will sound hollow.

Serve freshly baked, cut into thick slices and lavished with butter and jam. Spotted Dog is also really good eaten with cheese.

Stripy Cat

When Paul and Jeannie Rankin taught at the school some years ago, their two eldest children were in the kitchen with me while I was making Spotted Dog. They asked me if I ever used chocolate instead of sultanas in my Spotted Dog. Always happy to try anything once, so in went some chocolate chips. Once it was out of the oven and by all accounts a success, I asked the girls what should I call it. 'Stripy Cat, of course,' they declared in unison. So Stripy Cat was born.

Makes: 1 loaf

Cooking time: 45 minutes, approximately

What you need:
- 450 g/1 lb plain white flour, preferably unbleached
- 1 level teaspoon salt
- 1 level teaspoon bread soda, finely sieved
- 1 dessertspoon sugar
- 85–110 g/3–4 oz dark chocolate, roughly chopped
- 350 ml/12 fl oz buttermilk, approximately
- 1 egg

What you do: Fully preheat your oven to 220°C/425°F/regulo 7.

Just the same as when making Spotted Dog, sieve the flour into a large mixing bowl and add the bread soda. Add the salt, sugar and chocolate. Mix the ingredients together by hand by lifting them up high and then letting them fall back into the bowl through your fingers to add more air and make your bread lighter.

Once the dry ingredients are well mixed together, follow the steps given in the Spotted Dog recipe.

Serve this delicious sweet bread freshly baked, cut into thick slices and generously smeared with butter.

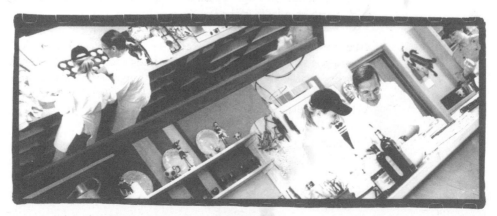

Brown Soda Bread

'I would simply love to be able to make a loaf of Brown Soda Bread,' said Sinead Cusack wistfully at a lunch party in west Cork last summer. My ears pricked up. The next day Sinead and her son Max were elbow deep in flour in the kitchen of the cottage we had rented outside Durrus. The fun of baking and the excitement of taking your first loaf of bread out of the oven is the same for everyone.

Makes: One large loaf

Cooking time: 40–55 minutes

What you need:
- 570 g/1¼ lb brown wholemeal flour
- 570 g/1¼ lb plain white flour
- 2 rounded teaspoons of salt
- 2 rounded teaspoons bread soda, finely sieved
- 850 ml/1½ pints buttermilk, approximately

What you do: Fully preheat the oven to 230°C/450°F/regulo 8.

Mix the flours, salt and bread soda together in a large, wide bowl.

Pour most of the milk into the middle of the flour. Using your hand with the fingers open and stiff, mix the ingredients in a full circle drawing in the flour from the sides of the bowl, adding more milk if necessary, until the dough is softish, but not too wet.

Turn out the dough onto a well-floured work surface. Then wash and dry your hands.

Tidy up the dough by lightly rolling it around with lightly floured hands. Then pat it gently into a round about 6 cm/2 in high.

Place the dough on a lightly floured baking sheet, cut it across and prick it with your knife in the usual way.

Bake in the fully preheated oven for 15–20 minutes and then reduce the temperature to 200°C/400°F/regulo 6 for a further 20–25 minutes. Turn the bread upside down on the baking sheet for 5–10 minutes before the end of baking. When the bread is cooked it will sound hollow when tapped.

Cool on a wire rack.

Timmy's Brown Bread

The ultimate food combination for me is a freshly laid free-range egg, soft-boiled, and a slice of generously buttered brown bread. Nothing can compete with the sheer ease and beauty of this meal.

Brown soda bread is one of things I miss most when I am abroad. When my daughter Lydia returned from a year travelling and working in Australia, the one thing she wanted to eat when she came home was my brown soda bread. For many Irish emigrants brown soda bread is a real taste of home.

Makes: 1 loaf

Cooking time: 35 minutes, approximately

What you need:
- 225 g/8 oz plain white flour
- 225 g/8 oz brown wholemeal flour
- 50 g/2 oz kibbled wheat
- 50 g/2 oz granary flour
- 2–3 teaspoons sesame seeds
- 1 rounded teaspoon brown sugar
- 1 rounded teaspoon salt
- 1 level teaspoon bread soda, finely sieved
- 1 small egg
- 15 g/$\frac{1}{2}$ oz butter
- 350 ml/12 fl oz buttermilk, approximately

What you do: Fully preheat the oven to 230°C/450°F/regulo 8.

In a large bowl mix the brown flour, white flour, kibbled wheat, granary flour, sesame seeds, sugar, salt and bread soda together. Rub in the butter.

Make a well in the centre of the dry ingredients.

Break the egg into the bottom of your measuring jug and add the buttermilk to the 400 ml/14 fl oz line, with the egg forming part of your total liquid measurement. Pour most of this milk and egg mixture into the flour. Using one hand, with the fingers open and stiff, as usual when making any soda bread, mix in a full circle drawing in the flour from the sides of the bowl, adding more milk and egg if necessary.

Avoid over-mixing, keep the dough light and airy. When soft, but not too sticky, turn out the dough onto a well-floured work surface. Wash and dry your hands.

Tidy gently around the edges. Then pat down to about 6 cm/2 in high.

Place the dough on a lightly floured baking sheet and cut a deep cross in it, letting the cuts go right over the sides of the bread. And remember to let the fairies out before baking by pricking the dough with your knife!

Bake in the fully preheated oven for about 15 minutes and then reduce the temperature to 200°C/400°F/regulo 6 for about a further 20 minutes. Tap the bread to check it is cooked, and leave to cool on a wire rack.

Seedy Bread

If you like caraway seeds, this is a must, delicious served for afternoon tea.

Makes:	1 loaf
Cooking time:	40 minutes, approximately
What you need:	• 450 g/1 lb plain white flour, preferably unbleached • 1 level teaspoon salt • 1 level teaspoon bread soda, finely sieved • 1 tablespoon sugar • 2–3 teaspoons caraway seeds • 20 g/$\frac{3}{4}$ oz butter, optional • 400 ml/14 fl oz buttermilk, approximately
What you do:	First fully preheat the oven to 230°C/450°F/regulo 8.

Sieve the flour, salt and bread soda into a large, wide mixing bowl. Add the caraway seeds. Rub in the butter if you are including it.

Now follow the steps as for the basic soda bread given in full on page 2.

When you are ready to bake your bread, place the dough in the preheated oven for 15 minutes, then turn down the heat to 200°C/400°F/regulo 6 and bake for a further 25 minutes, or until just cooked. If you are in doubt, tap the bottom of the bread. When cooked, it will sound hollow.

Ardsallagh Goat's Milk Loaf

This bread was discovered quite by accident when some goat's milk was left out on the counter one warm afternoon. Rather than throw it out I used it to make a loaf of soda bread. The soured goat's milk was thinner than the commercially produced buttermilk normally used when making soda bread. As a result, the dough was quite wet and sloppy so I poured it into an oiled loaf tin — and Wow! a new, quick and easy bread was born!

Makes: 1 loaf

Cooking time: 65 minutes, approximately

What you need:
- 450 g/1 lb cream flour
- 1 level teaspoon bread soda
- 1 level teaspoon salt
- 400 ml/14 fl oz soured goat's milk

Topping:
- sunflower or sesame seeds, or any other seeds of your choice

What you do: First, fully preheat the oven to 230°C/450°F/regulo 8.

Sieve the flour, salt and bread soda into a large, wide mixing bowl.

Make a well in the centre. Pour all of the soured goat's milk into the flour. Using one hand with the fingers open and stiff, mix in a full circle drawing in the flour from the sides of the bowl, adding more milk if necessary.

In contrast to the softish, not too sticky dough that I usually aim for when making soda bread, this goat's milk dough should be very soft and too wet to knead.

Pour the dough into your oiled loaf tin, and sprinkle the top with sunflower seeds or the seeds of your choice.

Put your loaf in the preheated oven for 55 minutes, then turn out of the tin and put it straight back into the oven for a further 10 minutes, or until fully cooked. Check that it is cooked by tapping it and listening for the hollow sound.

Treacle Bread

If you want a quick, rich bread to have with afternoon tea, try this.

Makes:	1 loaf
Cooking time:	35 minutes, approximately

What you need:
- 450 g/1 lb plain white flour, preferably unbleached
- 1 level teaspoon salt
- 1 level teaspoon bread soda, finely sieved
- 400 ml/14 fl oz buttermilk, approximately
- 2 tablespoons treacle

What you do: Fully preheat the oven to 230°C/450°F/regulo 8.

Sieve the flour, salt and bread soda into a large, wide mixing bowl. Make a well in the centre.

In a measuring jug, add the treacle to the buttermilk.

Pour most of the milk into the flour. Using the usual soda bread technique, one hand with the fingers open and stiff, mix the ingredients in a full circle, drawing in the flour from the sides of the bowl and adding more milk if necessary.

Make the dough softish and not wet, in the usual way, mixing it as quickly and as gently as possible to keep it light and airy. When the dough all comes together, turn it out onto a well-floured work surface. Wash and dry your hands.

Roll the dough around gently with floury hands for a few seconds, just enough to tidy it up. Then pat it gently into a round about 6 cm/2 in high.

Place the dough on a lightly floured baking sheet, and with a sharp knife cut a deep cross, letting the cuts go right over the sides. Then prick the dough.

Put your treacle loaf into the preheated oven for 10 minutes, then turn down the oven to 200°C/400°F/regulo 6 and cook for about 25 minutes more until cooked. Tap the loaf to check for the hollow sound that says 'I'm ready.'

Gubeen Crispy Bacon Bread

We have our own organically raised, saddleback pigs on our farm. Fingal Ferguson of Gubeen, Schull, West Cork, had begun his own smokehouse. So we started by sending him one of our pigs, and he sent us back the most delicious smoked bacon, salami and chorizo sausage. We sent him another, and then another, and back would come the bacon, each time a slightly different recipe until Fingal was happy with the cure or we had run out of pigs!

This recipe is always best with home-cured bacon.

Makes:	1 loaf
Cooking time:	35 minutes, approximately
What you need:	• 450 g/1 lb plain white flour, preferably unbleached • 1 level teaspoon salt • 1 level teaspoon bread soda, finely sieved • 85–110 g/3–4 oz of cooked crispy bacon • 400 ml/14 fl oz buttermilk, approximately
What you do:	First, fully preheat the oven to 230°C/450°F/regulo 8. Sieve the flour, salt and bread soda into a large, wide mixing bowl. Make a well in the centre. Cut the bacon into lardons 5 mm/$\frac{1}{2}$ in thick. Fry the bacon in a hot pan until crisp. To include the bacon and its fat in the measuring, put it into your measuring jug and then pour the buttermilk in and bring it up to the 400 ml/14 fl oz mark. Now you can follow the rest of the basic soda bread steps given on page 2. Place your loaf into the preheated oven for 10 minutes, then turn the oven down to 200°C/400°F/regulo 6 for 25 minutes or until it is just cooked, and sounds hollow when you tap it.

Yellow Meal Griddle Bread

If you are a polenta lover this bread is for you. It is easy and probably one of the fastest breads in the book!

Makes: One griddle loaf

Cooking time: 7–8 minutes

What you need:
- 110 g/4 oz yellow meal
- good pinch of salt
- $\frac{1}{4}$ teaspoon bread soda, finely sieved
- 175 ml/6 fl oz buttermilk
- knob of butter

What you do: Put the yellow meal, salt and sieved bread soda in your bowl and add the buttermilk. Beat the mixture well with a wooden spoon for 4–5 minutes.

Thoroughly heat a non-stick pan, then add the knob of butter. Carefully pour the batter into the pan. Cook for 4–5 minutes, when little bubbles begin to form on the surface of the batter, it is ready to be turned over. Gently and carefully flip the bread over.

Cook for a further 3 minutes.

Cut into slices and serve with soft butter and crispy back rashers.

Potato Bread

This bread often accompanies a traditional Irish fried breakfast.

Makes:	1 loaf
Cooking time:	30 minutes, approximately
What you need:	• 50 g/2 oz flour
	• 2 teaspoons salt
	• 2 teaspoons baking powder
	• 225 g/8 oz cooked mashed potatoes
	• 25 g/1 oz butter, melted
What you do:	Fully preheat the oven to 180°C/350°F/regulo 4.

Into a large, wide mixing bowl, sieve the flour, salt and baking powder together. Add the potatoes. Melt the butter and pour it in.

Knead lightly and roll out the dough, then cut it in four. Bake on a greased baking sheet in the preheated oven for approximately 30 minutes or until golden.

Introduction to
Scones

Scones and sweet breads have always been a firm favourite with almost everybody, but with life moving so fast it's easy to forget how simple and quick it is to bake your own yummy scones either to eat yourself or to share with friends. Everything in this chapter, whether sweet or savoury, can be ready to eat in under an hour.

People are always amazed at just how easy baking a scone really is. A young friend, Sara, was in the kitchen the other day when I was making my sweet white scones, and while we chatted I had the scones made and in and out of the oven. She was totally stunned. Within just 20 minutes of her arrival we were sitting down to tea and home-made scones. My friend went back to Dublin full of enthusiasm and determination to bake scones for her house mates and start a mini revolution.

The pleasure we all feel when offering our own home baking to a friend with their cup of tea is indescribable.

In the following pages I will show you just how easy it is to bake both sweet and savoury scones, and also crumpets and other yummies. I hope to be able to prove to you that in the time it takes to watch your favourite soap opera you could have made something tasty to eat! **Do it at the same time!**

When following these recipes, there are a few points to keep in mind:

- Always make sure your oven is up to temperature.
- Choose a large mixing bowl.
- Be sure to measure your ingredients carefully.
- If using bread soda, sieve it finely.
- When making scones, make sure the butter is well chilled.
- *Start your own scone revolution!*

Grandma's Sweet White Scones

My earliest memory of visiting my mother-in-law, Mrs Elizabeth O'Connell, in Cullohill Co. Laois, was of her serving up these delicious scones with home-made raspberry jam (see page 140) and whipped cream.

The trick to these sweet white scones is to make sure the butter is really chilled so that it breaks and crumbles into the flour to give the scones their extra special light texture.

Makes: 16

Cooking time: 15 minutes, approximately

What you need:
- 450 g/1 lb plain white flour
- 3 rounded teaspoons baking powder
- pinch of salt
- 25 g/1 oz castor sugar
- 85 g/3 oz butter, chilled
- 2 medium eggs
- 200–225 ml/7—8 fl oz fresh milk

Topping:
- egg wash
- 50 g/2 oz granulated sugar

What you do: Fully preheat the oven to 250°C/475°F/regulo 9.

Into a large, wide bowl, sieve the flour, baking powder and salt together. Add the castor sugar. Cut the chilled butter into cubes. Then rub the butter into the dry ingredients. Make a well in the centre.

Break the eggs into a measuring jug and whisk lightly. Add the milk, bringing the liquid up to the 300 ml/10 fl oz mark. Pour nearly all of the milk and egg mixture into the flour. Using one hand with the fingers open and stiff, mix in a full circle drawing in the flour from the sides of the bowl, adding more milk and egg if necessary. Bring the ingredients gently together into a soft dough.

Turn the dough out onto a floured work surface.

Gently roll out the scone dough into a rectangle about 2 cm/$\frac{3}{4}$ in high. Using a metal dough cutter lightly dusted with flour, cut the scone dough into about 16 scones, about 4 cm/1$\frac{1}{2}$ in round. To prevent the scones toppling over while baking, cut quickly and sharply downwards with the dough cutter.

Get two deep saucers. Into the first pour in the egg wash; into the second put in the granulated sugar. First brush the scones with the egg wash, then dip the scones into the granulated sugar.

Place the scones on a lightly floured baking sheet sugar side up. Bake them in your preheated oven for 5 minutes then turn the heat down to 230°C/450°F/regulo 8 and bake for a further 10 minutes. Cool on a wire rack.

Eat spread with butter and raspberry jam. Or, if you feel really decadent, spread a little raspberry jam and top with whipped cream.

Sultana Scones

My daughter Lydia found this recipe ideal when she worked as a chalet girl in Verbier because unlike the traditional sweet scone recipe these can be made ahead as the fruit keeps them fresh. Lydia was able to make them first thing in the morning and then have some time to ski before nipping back to her chalet to serve her guests an afternoon tea of sultana scones.

Makes:	16
Cooking time:	15 minutes, approximately
What you need:	• 450 g/1 lb plain white flour
	• 3 rounded teaspoons baking powder
	• pinch of salt
	• 25 g/1 oz castor sugar
	• 85 g/3 oz butter, chilled
	• 85–110 g/3–4 oz sultanas
	• 2 medium eggs
	• 200–225 ml/7–8 fl oz fresh milk

Topping:
- egg wash
- 50 g/2 oz granulated sugar

What you do: Preheat the oven to 250°C/475°F/regulo 9.

These scones are based on the recipe for Grandma's Sweet White Scones.

Once you have sieved the flour, baking powder and salt together, add in the castor sugar. Cut the chilled butter into cubes and rub the butter into the dry ingredients. Then mix in your sultanas.

On reaching this stage, you should follow the steps on page 16 to prepare your scone dough, then, as before, first brush the scones with the egg wash, then dip them into the granulated sugar to create a tasty sweet topping.

Place the scones on a lightly floured baking sheet sugar side up in your preheated oven for 5 minutes. Turn down the heat to 230°C/450°F/regulo 8 and bake for a further 10 minutes. Cool on a wire rack.

Serve, spread generously with butter.

Chocolate Chip Scones

This my quick version of the popular French snack for children, yummy chocolate bread.

Makes: 16

Cooking time: 15 minutes, approximately

What you need:
- 450 g/1 lb plain white flour
- 3 rounded teaspoons baking powder
- pinch of salt
- 25 g/1 oz castor sugar
- 85 g/3 oz butter, chilled
- 85–110 g/3–4 oz dark chocolate, roughly chopped
- 2 medium eggs
- 200–225 ml/7–8 fl oz fresh milk

Topping:
- egg wash

The beginning of it all

Selection of Soda Breads

Orange Butter Scones

Coffee and Walnut Scones

Crunchy Tops

Teeny, Weeny, Spicy Cheese and Onion Scones

Scrummy Brown Buns

What you do: Preheat the oven to 250°C/475°F/regulo 9.

Sieve the flour, baking powder and salt together into a large, wide plastic bowl. Add in the castor sugar. Cut the chilled butter into cubes. Rub the butter into the dry ingredients. Mix in the chocolate.

Prepare the scone dough by following the basic sweet white scones recipe on page 16.

Brush the scones with your egg wash. Then place them on a lightly floured baking sheet.

Put the scones into the preheated oven for 5 minutes, then turn down the heat to 230°C/450°F/regulo 8 to bake for a further 10 minutes. Cool on a wire rack.

Orange Butter Scones

Make sure you have an audience when taking these scones out of the oven and wait for the ooh's and aah's as all the swirls will have merged together.

These scones are super served on their own or with a little whipped cream on the side. They make an ideal snack for a packed lunch as you don't need to butter them.

Makes: 14

Cooking time: 15 minutes, approximately

What you need:
- 450 g/1 lb plain white flour
- 3 rounded teaspoons baking powder
- pinch of salt
- 25 g/1 oz castor sugar
- 85 g/3 oz butter, chilled
- 2 medium eggs
- 200–225 ml/7–8 fl oz fresh milk

Orange butter:
- 2 oranges, finely grated zest
- 85 g/3 oz butter
- 100 g/$3\frac{1}{2}$ oz icing sugar, sieved

What you need: **Topping:**
- egg wash
- 50 g/2 oz granulated sugar

What you do: Fully preheat the oven to 250°C/475°F/regulo 9.

Prepare the orange butter in advance. Cream the butter with the finely grated orange zest, add the sieved icing sugar and beat together until light and fluffy.

To make the scone dough, follow the steps as described for the basic recipe on page 16.

When you have mixed the dough, turn it out onto a very well-floured work surface. Knead lightly, just enough to bring together.

Now gently roll the scone dough into a rectangle about 2 cm/$\frac{3}{4}$ in high and about 35 x 23 cm/14 x 9 in. Using a plastic spatula, spread the orange butter over the top surface of the dough. Gently roll up the dough as you would roll a Swiss roll.

With a sharp, metal dough cutter lightly dusted with flour, cut the rolled scone dough into about 14 slices.

Place the scones cut side down on a lightly floured baking sheet. First brush the scones with the egg wash, then sprinkle over the top with granulated sugar.

Put the scones into your preheated oven to bake for 5 minutes then turn down the heat to 230°C/450°F/regulo 8 and leave to bake for a further 10 minutes.

Cool on a wire rack. Then tuck in!

Coffee and Walnut Scones

These are a really quick and easy scone to serve with afternoon tea. Instead of baking a cake, you can have these scones ready from start to finish in under half an hour. As everyone is getting busier and busier these days, it is great to have a few staple recipes that can be made with very little effort and even less time. So no excuse for not baking!

Makes: 16

Cooking time: 15 minutes, approximately

What you need:
- 450 g/1 lb plain white flour
- 3 teaspoons baking powder
- pinch of salt
- 25 g/1 oz castor sugar
- 85 g/3 oz butter, chilled
- 70 g/$2\frac{1}{2}$ oz walnuts, coarsely chopped
- 2 medium eggs
- 175–200 ml/6–7 fl oz fresh milk
- 1–2 tablespoons coffee essence

Coffee icing:
- 210 g/$7\frac{1}{2}$ oz icing sugar
- 1 tablespoon coffee essence
- 2 tablespoons boiling water

What you do: Fully preheated the oven 250°C/475°F/regulo 9.

Into your large, plastic mixing bowl, sieve the flour, baking powder and salt together. Add the castor sugar. Cut the chilled butter into cubes. Rub the butter into the dry ingredients. Mix in the chopped walnuts. Make a well in the centre.

Break the eggs into a measuring jug and whisk lightly, add the coffee essence and then enough milk to bring the liquid measurement up to the 300 ml/10 fl oz mark. Pour nearly all of this milk, egg and coffee mixture into the flour.

Using your hand with fingers open and stiff, mix the ingredients in a full circle drawing in the flour from the sides of the bowl, adding more liquid if necessary. Bring the dough gently together to a soft consistency.

Turn the dough out onto a floured work surface. Pat it lightly, just enough to bring it together.

Gently roll out the scone dough into a rectangle about 2 cm/$\frac{3}{4}$ in high. With a metal dough cutter lightly dusted with flour cut the scone dough into about 16 scones each about 4 cm/$1\frac{1}{2}$ in across.

Place the scones on a lightly floured baking sheet and bake in the preheated oven for 5 minutes, then turn down the heat to 230°C/450°F/regulo 8 and bake for a further 5–10 minutes. Cool on a wire tray.

While the scones are cooking, make the coffee icing. Sieve the icing sugar into a medium-sized mixing bowl. Add the coffee essence and whisk in the boiling water a tablespoon at a time.

Whisk the icing till silky and smooth. How thick a consistency you make the icing is very much down to personal preference, but it is generally best if it is not too runny.

When the scones have cooled, spread the top of each scone generously with the icing.

Kibbled Wheat and Oatmeal Scones

These nutty, light scones always prove popular when served with mature cheddar cheese and Ballymaloe Relish, one of the many food marriages made in heaven.

Makes:	8–10 scones
Cooking time:	20–25 minutes

What you need:
- 285 g/10 oz brown wholemeal flour
- 225 g/8 oz plain white flour
- 25 g/1 oz oatmeal
- 25 g/1 oz kibbled wheat
- 1 rounded teaspoon salt
- 1 rounded teaspoon bread soda, finely sieved
- 25 g/1 oz butter
- 1 egg, preferably free-range
- 425 ml/15 fl oz buttermilk

Topping:
- 25 g/1 oz kibbled wheat
- 25 g/1 oz oatmeal

What you do: First, fully preheat the oven to 230°C/450°F/regulo 8.

In a large, wide bowl mix together the flours, oatmeal, kibbled wheat, salt and finely sieved bread soda.

Rub in the butter. Make a well in the centre. Whisk the egg and, keeping a little back for the top, pour the rest of the egg into a measuring jug. Bring the liquid up to the 425 ml/15 fl oz mark with the buttermilk.

Pour most of the liquid into the flour. Using one hand with the fingers open and stiff, mix in a full circle, drawing in the flour from the sides of the bowl, adding more milk and egg mixture if necessary.

The dough should be softish, not too wet and sticky. Mix as quickly and gently as possible, keeping it light and airy. When the dough comes together, turn out onto a well-floured work surface. Wash and dry your hands.

With floured hands, roll the dough lightly for a few seconds, just enough to shape it into a square. Flatten slightly to about 4 cm/$1\frac{1}{2}$ in high.

Cut the dough into square scones. Brush the top of the dough with the beaten egg, adding a little extra buttermilk if needed. On a flat plate, mix the topping of kibbled wheat and oatmeal and dip each scone into this mixture.

Transfer the scones to a lightly floured baking sheet. Bake for about 15 minutes, then reduce the heat to 200°C/400°F/regulo 6 for another 5–10 minutes, depending on their size. When cooked, they should sound hollow when tapped. Cool on a wire rack.

Herb and Cheese Scones

A quick, tasty, last-minute accompaniment to any soup, based on the soda bread technique. You can really use your imagination and vary the herbs. Any leftover scones can be popped into the freezer for a future emergency.

Makes:	16
Cooking time:	15 minutes, approximately
What you need:	• 450 g/1 lb plain white flour, preferably unbleached • 1 level teaspoon salt • 1 level teaspoon bread soda, finely sieved • 1 dessertspoon each of freshly chopped rosemary, sage and chives • 400 ml/14 fl oz buttermilk, approximately • 50 g/2 oz cheddar cheese, finely grated
What you do:	Preheat the oven to 230°C/450°F/regulo 8.

Sieve the flour, salt and bread soda into a large, wide mixing bowl. Add your chosen freshly chopped herbs to the dry ingredients. Make a well in the centre.

Pour most of the buttermilk into the flour. Using our usual technique, one hand with fingers open and stiff, mix the ingredients in a full circle, drawing in the flour from the sides of the bowl. Add more milk if necessary, keeping a little bit back for the top, so that the dough is softish and not too wet.

Avoid over-mixing the dough. Mix it quickly and keep it light and airy. Turn out onto a well-floured work surface. Wash and dry your hands.

With floury hands, shape the dough gently into a square. Pat down lightly to about 4 cm/$1\frac{1}{2}$ in deep.

Cut the dough into square scones. Brush the top of the dough with a little extra buttermilk. Put the grated cheddar cheese on a flat plate and dip each scone into the cheese.

Transfer the scones to a lightly floured baking sheet and bake in the preheated oven for about 15 minutes, depending on the size of the scones. To check whether they are cooked, tap them and they will sound hollow. Take out and cool on a wire rack.

Crunchy Tops

These crunchy-topped scones join to make a full loaf. With surprisingly little effort you can create a stunning effect with the toppings you choose. The scones are so attractive and often look a bit like a patchwork quilt when they come out of the oven.

Makes: 7

Cooking time: 25–30 minutes

What you need:
- 450 g/1 lb plain white flour, preferably unbleached
- 1 level teaspoon salt
- 1 level teaspoon bread soda, finely sieved
- 400 ml/14 fl oz buttermilk

- 1 round tin, 23 cm/9 in across, 4 cm/1$\frac{1}{2}$ in deep, well-greased with oil or butter

Topping:
- egg wash
- herbs and seeds of your choice: for example, sunflower seeds, sesame seeds, kibbled wheat, caraway seeds, poppy seeds, oat flakes; and grated mature cheddar cheese

What you do: Preheat the oven to 230°C/450°F/regulo 8.

Into a large mixing bowl, sieve the flour, salt and bread soda. Make a well in the centre.

Pour most of the buttermilk into the flour. Mix a softish dough using one hand with the fingers open and stiff, mix in a full circle drawing in the flour from the sides of the bowl, adding more buttermilk if necessary. Avoid over-mixing to keep the dough light.

Turn the dough out onto a well-floured surface. Wash and dry your hands.

Gently tidy up the dough and pat it down into a round about 4 cm/1$\frac{1}{2}$ in high.

Using a 7.5 cm/3 in scone cutter, stamp out 6 scones. Bring the rest of the dough together to make one more scone.

Brush the top of each scone with a little egg wash. Dip each one in the toppings of your choice. Arrange side by side in a well-greased tin.

Bake in the fully preheated oven for 25–30 minutes, or until fully cooked. Test for that hollow sound to check when they are ready. Remove from the tin and allow to cool on a wire tray.

Teeny, Weeny, Spicy Cheese and Onion Scones

These scones are made with cayenne pepper to give them a real kick. Try eating them with a soft creamy goat's cheese. They are ideal for serving as a canapé with drinks. The scones freeze very well and will defrost within about half an hour so they are a great stand-by. It's especially handy to keep some frozen around Christmas time for those unexpected guests that arrive on your doorstep calling in with Christmas cheer.

Makes: about 50

Cooking time: 10–12 minutes

What you need:
- 2 tablespoons olive oil
- 2 medium onions, very finely chopped
- 450 g/1 lb plain flour
- 3 teaspoons baking powder
- 1 teaspoon salt
- 1 rounded teaspoon English mustard powder
- 1 level teaspoon cayenne pepper
- 1 teaspoon freshly ground black pepper
- 50 g/2 oz butter
- 40 g/1½ oz Parmesan cheese
- 40 g/1½ oz mature cheddar cheese
- 225 ml/8 fl oz milk
- 1 large egg

- 2 baking sheets, lightly oiled

Topping:
- egg wash
- 25 g/1 oz Parmesan cheese

What you do: Fully preheat the oven to 200°C/400°F/regulo 6.

In a large heavy-based frying pan, heat the olive oil. Add the finely chopped onions. Cook on a high heat for about 10 minutes, stirring frequently. The onions need to be just beginning to turn a golden colour and have started to caramelise around the edges. Turn out onto a plate and leave to cool.

While the onions are cooling sieve the flour, baking powder, salt, mustard and cayenne pepper into a large, wide mixing bowl. Add the freshly ground black pepper and rub in the butter. Stir in the freshly grated cheeses and the onions. Combine all these ingredients thoroughly together.

Beat the egg in a bowl and add it to the milk. Make a well in the centre of the flour, cheese and onion mixture and then pour in almost all of the liquid. Using one hand with your fingers open and stiff, mix in a full circle, drawing in the flour from the sides of the bowl, adding more of the liquid if necessary. Bring gently together into a soft dough.

Turn the dough out onto a floured work surface. Pat lightly, just enough to tidy the dough.

Gently press the scone dough into a rectangle about 2.5 cm/1 in high. Paint the dough with egg wash and scatter the grated Parmesan cheese on top. With a metal dough cutter divide the dough into teeny scones, about 2.5 cm/1 in square.

Place the scones, cheese side up, on a lightly oiled and floured baking sheet. Bake in the preheated oven for 10–12 minutes. Then allow to cool on a wire rack.

Rachel's Chocolate Crumpets

Here is a quick and easy crowd-pleasing recipe developed by my daughter-in-law Rachel. These scrummy crumpets are ideal to serve at a children's party. You can be sure they will be eaten as fast as you can cook them. And they go down just as well with grown ups at any party!

Makes:	10–12
Cooking time:	5–10 minutes
What you need:	• 225 g/8 oz flour
	• pinch of salt
	• $\frac{1}{2}$ level teaspoon bread soda, finely sieved
	• 25 g/1 oz butter
	• 1 tablespoon castor sugar
	• 85 g/3 oz chocolate, roughly chopped
	• 2 eggs
	• 175 ml/6 fl oz buttermilk

What you do: Into a large, wide mixing bowl, sieve the flour, bread soda and salt. Rub in the butter. Stir in the castor sugar and the roughly chopped chocolate.

Make a well in the centre of the dry ingredients.

Crack the egg into a measuring jug, whisk lightly to break up the yolk, then add the buttermilk to bring the liquid measurement up to the 300 ml/10 fl oz level. Pour nearly all of the milk and egg mixture into the flour.

Using one hand with the fingers open and stiff, mix in a full circle drawing in the flour from the sides of the bowl, adding more milk if necessary. Bring gently together into a thick batter, far too wet to knead.

Heat a non-stick pan on the hob. There is no need to grease it. Keep the pan on a very low heat and gently drop a heaped tablespoon of the batter into the pan. When bubbles start to form on the surface, turn the crumpet over, it will be golden brown on the underside. Cook for a further 5 minutes.

Serve straight from the pan spread with delicious soft butter.

Cinnamon Pancakes

My own version of the traditional buttermilk pancake. We eat them hot straight from the pan with melted butter and cinnamon sugar. They are also super with crispy bacon and maple syrup.

Makes: 8–10

Cooking time: just a few minutes

What you need:
- 225 ml/8 fl oz buttermilk
- 85 g/3 oz butter
- 110 g/4 oz flour
- $\frac{1}{2}$ teaspoon salt
- 1 teaspoon bread soda, finely sieved
- 2 teaspoons freshly ground cinnamon
- 1 egg

To serve:
- butter
- castor sugar mixed with ground cinnamon

What you do: In a mixing bowl combine the buttermilk, egg and melted butter. Whisk thoroughly until the mixture is smooth and well blended.

In another bowl sieve the flour, salt, cinnamon and bread soda. Stir the flour mixture into the liquid until just moistened. Strange as this sounds, leave any lumps of flour in the mixture.

Heat a non-stick frying pan to medium heat. Spoon out about 2 tablespoons of batter for each pancake. Cook until there are a few bubbles breaking on the surface. Gently turn the pancake over — it will be golden brown underneath. Cook briefly on the other side.

Serve warm, spread with melted butter and sprinkled with cinnamon castor sugar.

American Popovers

One of my all-time favourite childhood recipes. Popovers are ideal for just about any occasion and still served as a lunch-time dessert at Ballymaloe, with raspberry jam, softly whipped cream and a dusting of icing sugar.

Makes:	14
Cooking time:	20 minutes, approximately
What you need:	• 110 g/4 oz plain flour
	• 2 eggs
	• 300 ml/10 fl oz milk
	• 15 g/$\frac{1}{2}$ oz butter, melted
	• 1 bun tray
	Filling:
	• home-made raspberry jam (see page 140)
	• whipped cream
What you do:	Preheat the oven to 230°C/450°F/regulo 8.

Into a large, wide mixing bowl sieve the flour, make a well in the centre and drop in the eggs.

Using a whisk, stir constantly, gradually bringing in the flour from the sides of the bowl.

Start to add the milk in a steady flow. When all the flour has been mixed in, whisk in the melted butter.

Cover and allow the mixture to stand for 1 hour.

Oil your bun tray. Put the tray into the preheated oven and when the oil is starting to smoke, carefully remove the tray from the oven.

Quickly, half-fill each mould with the batter and bake for 20 minutes.

Remove from the oven and take the buns out of the tray. Place on a wire rack to cool.

Serve with home-made raspberry jam and softly whipped cream.

Brownies

The all-American favourite. I cannot stress enough how crucial it is to use the correct size tin for this recipe. It will not work otherwise. And you need to keep your nerve when removing the brownies from the oven as the mixture will still be soft in the centre. It will set as it cools but should remain moist even when cold.

Makes:	16
Cooking time:	35 minutes, approximately
What you need:	• 85–110 g/3–4 oz dark chocolate
	• 100 g/$3\frac{1}{2}$ oz butter
	• 200 g/7 oz castor sugar
	• 2 eggs
	• $\frac{1}{2}$ teaspoon of vanilla extract
	• 85 g/3 oz plain flour
	• 1 level teaspoon baking powder
	• pinch of salt
	• 110 g/4 oz pecan nuts, roughly chopped
	• 1 square baking tin, 20 cm/8 in, lined with parchment paper
What you do:	Fully preheat the oven to 180°C/350°F/regulo 4.

Half-fill a saucepan with water and bring to the boil. Put a Pyrex bowl over the pan of water, making sure the base of the bowl does not touch the water. Turn off the heat under the saucepan. Put the chocolate in the bowl and leave it to melt.

Using a food-mixer, cream the butter and sugar till light and fluffy. Beat in the lightly whisked eggs and the vanilla essence.

Stir in the melted chocolate. Gently fold in the flour, salt and chopped nuts.

Spread the mixture into the prepared tin. Bake in the preheated oven for 35 minutes.

Allow to cool. Then cut into squares.

The brownies are great served slightly warm with a scoop of vanilla ice cream (see page 147 for my Ballymaloe Vanilla Ice Cream recipe).

Balloons

Always a great favourite for children's tea at Ballymaloe, balloons are similar in taste to doughnuts, and take just minutes to prepare. The only problem you will have with these is being able keep up with the demand!

Makes:	12–15 balloons
Cooking time:	6–8 minutes

What you need:
- 140 g/5 oz plain flour
- 2 teaspoons castor sugar
- pinch of salt
- 1 teaspoon baking powder
- 170 ml/6 fl oz milk

- oil for deep frying

Topping:
- 3 tablespoons castor sugar mixed with 1 tablespoon ground cinnamon

What you do: Heat the oil in a deep-fat fryer to 180°C/350°F. Into a large mixing bowl, sieve the dry ingredients together.

Make a well in the centre and mix to a thick batter with the milk.

Take a teaspoon of the mixture and push it gently off the spoon with another spoon close to the surface of the oil so that it slides in a round ball into the hot oil. Be careful!

Repeat this with the rest of the batter and fry until golden, for about 6–8 minutes.

Remove the balloons from the oil, drain on kitchen paper and roll them in the cinnamon sugar. Serve while still warm.

Introduction to Yeast

People are frequently put off at the thought of using yeast. *Don't be*. Sure, yeast bread takes longer to make than many other breads, but I will let you in on a little secret, it is actually easier to make a yeast-based dough than a soda-based dough.

Why? For the simple reason that a yeast dough is far more forgiving. There are few things more satisfying than the process of kneading your dough, watching it rise and then the ultimate joy of taking your beautiful bread from the oven. Your whole house will be filled with that wonderful comforting scent of fresh bread.

Yeast is a living organism. Brought to life like any of the rest of us: with a little love, warmth, moisture and food. Once the yeast is happy it starts to purr like a kitten, multiplying itself in the process and producing bubbles of carbon dioxide. Yeast can be introduced to the flour in many ways, each to bring about a slightly different result when the bread is baked.

Using yeast

- When you are using yeast, try, if it all possible, to use fresh yeast.
- Fresh yeast is normally sponged, or dissolved, in tepid liquid. If just water is used, the yeast will dissolve but if the liquid contains sugar or treacle it will foam a little.
- Yeast keeps for a few weeks if kept well covered and refrigerated.
- Yeast also freezes well. I recommend that you freeze it in 25 g/1 oz pieces ready to use.

- In some recipes, Carta Musica, for example, I have broken my own rule and used fast-acting yeast for convenience and also to demonstrate this alternative method.
- If using dried yeast, as it tends to be stronger than fresh yeast, I would recommend using half the quantity stated in the recipe. For example, 25 g/1 oz of fresh yeast would be 15 g/$\frac{1}{2}$ oz of dried yeast.
- There are 2 ways to kill yeast — direct contact with salt, or heat above 45–50°C/120°F.

Why knead?

In the process of kneading you develop the gluten in the flour which helps to trap the carbon dioxide in the structure of the dough.

Pointers for kneading

- If kneading by hand, always ensure the work surface is clean and very lightly dusted with flour.
- Don't be tempted to use loads of extra flour, just use enough to stop the dough from sticking to the surface.
- There are no hard and fast rules about how long to knead for, some doughs just require more work. On average 10 minutes is usually what is required.
- Don't worry when you start to knead, there are many ways to work the dough. The important thing to remember is to stretch the dough.
- Start by pulling the dough, fold it in on itself, press it down onto the work surface. Push it away from you with the heel of your hand. Pull it back towards you folding it over on itself . You will soon develop your own vigorous rhythm.

- Feel the dough transform from a messy, sticky mass to a smooth, shiny, elastic cushion of dough — very sensuous. I used to describe my dough as being sensuous, like a women's breast but now, in the days of political correctness, I'm having to change my ways!

What is there to prove?

- Don't rush the first rising. The dough will rise in its own good time. As a rule of thumb, the longer it takes the better.
- The ideal proving temperature is 35–40°C/85–105°F.
- Use a ceramic or plastic bowl.
- If the bowl is cold, warm it slightly by rinsing out with warm water.
- If your dough is too dry, rub the bowl with olive oil.
- If your dough is too wet, dust the bowl with a little flour.
- When proving, the dough will need to be placed somewhere that is free from draughts.
- Always cover the dough when proving, otherwise a skin will form.
- The dough will double in size.
- To check if the dough is fully proved – a finger gently pushed into the dough, if it springs back it is still active. If the indent of your finger remains in place, the dough is ready.

Shaping your bread

- There are endless ways of shaping your yeast bread, from simple plaits to knots and little buns, or you can place the dough into a well-oiled bread tin.
- Handle the dough gently.
- Avoid over-handling.
- If you find the dough tightening, cover and let it rest for a few minutes.
- It is important to remember that for the second rising the dough must be placed in or on whatever it is going to be cooked in/on, for example, if it is plaits, buns or knots you will put them on an oiled baking sheet; a loaf will have its second proving in its loaf tin
- Don't be tempted to over prove as it can cause the bread to collapse when placed in the hot oven.

Ballymaloe Brown Yeast Bread

The Ballymaloe Brown Yeast Bread is the most emotive bread in the book for me. Why? Well it has always been there, one of my earliest memories as a child was sitting in the kitchen in Ballymaloe watching the bread rise beside our Aga. In later years, when I was in boarding school it was the regular parcels of Ballymaloe brown yeast bread, Imokilly cheddar cheese and tomato chutney that helped me and my siblings survive.

Now, as a father and in fact a grandfather, it is still a bread I often make. My children too love to munch on the same combination of brown bread, cheese and tomato chutney.

It's the easiest of all the yeast breads we make in the school. It is the first yeast bread we teach the students. It requires just a single rising and no kneading at all. I often replace the treacle with molasses to make an even more nutritious loaf.

Makes: 1 loaf

Cooking time: 45–50 minutes

What you need:
- 450 g/1 lb brown flour **or** 400 g/14 oz brown flour and 50 g/2 oz strong white flour
- 25 g/1 oz fresh yeast
- 425 ml/15 fl oz warm water
- 1 teaspoon black treacle
- 1 teaspoon salt
- sesame seeds, optional

What you do: Preheat oven to 230°C/450°F/regulo 8.

In a large, wide mixing bowl, combine the brown and the white flour, add the salt.

Sponge the yeast in 150 ml/5 fl oz of tepid water with the teaspoon of treacle, leave in a warm place for the yeast to become active, about 5 minutes.

Add the remaining water to the yeast and treacle mixture and stir well together. Pour this into the dry ingredients and mix with an open hand, drawing the flour from the sides of the bowl.

Mix to a wettish dough, too wet to knead. Pour into the lightly oiled 2lb loaf tin. Sprinkle the top with sesame seeds if you are using them.

Put the tin in a warm place, cover with a tea-towel. Leave for about 35–40 minutes. The bread will have risen to twice its original size. It should be just peeping above the rim.

Remove the tea-towel. Bake for 45–50 minutes, or until the bread looks nicely browned and sounds hollow when tapped.

I like to remove the bread from the tins about 10 minutes before the end of cooking and put it back into the oven, upside down, to crisp all round.

Light Sunny Brown Bread

A similar method to Ballymaloe Brown Yeast Bread, it also requires just a single rising and no kneading. Due to the higher proportion of white flour this bread is a big hit with the little ones. I find it a great way to introduce a little more fibre into a child's diet, especially a child who won't eat regular brown bread. The texture of this loaf is soft and light.

Makes:	1 loaf
Cooking time:	45–50 minutes
What you need:	• 400 g/14 oz strong white flour
	• 50 g/2 oz strong brown flour
	• 1 teaspoon salt
	• 25 g/1 oz fresh yeast
	• 400 ml/14 fl oz warm water
	• 2 teaspoons brown cane sugar
	• 25 g/1 oz sunflower seeds

What you do: Fully preheat oven to 230°C/450°F/regulo 8.

In a large, wide mixing bowl combine the brown and white flour, add the salt.

Sponge the yeast in 150 ml/5 fl oz of tepid water with the brown sugar and then leave in a warm place for the yeast to become active, about 5 minutes.

Add the remaining water to the yeast and sugar and stir well. Pour the liquid into the dry ingredients and mix with an open hand, drawing the flour from the sides of the bowl.

Mix to a wettish dough that is too wet to knead.

Oil the loaf tin and sprinkle the base with a single layer of sunflower seeds. Pour in the dough.

Put the tin in a warm place and cover with a tea-towel. Leave for about 30–40 minutes approximately. The bread will have risen to twice its original size.

Remove the tea-towel. Bake for 45–50 minutes, or until the bread looks nicely browned and sounds hollow when tapped.

Scrummy Brown Buns

These stunning buns look truly amazing when served and your friends will assume they took at least 3 times the effort to make than they really did. The buns require no kneading at all and are ready for the oven after the first rising.

This will become a treasured recipe in your repertoire. You will wonder how you did without it!

Makes:	12
Cooking time:	25–30 minutes
What you need:	• 15 g/$\frac{1}{2}$ oz fresh yeast
	• 1 teaspoon of treacle
	• 325 ml/11 fl oz warm water
	• 170 g/6 oz strong white flour
	• 170 g/6 oz wholemeal flour
	• 1 teaspoon salt
	• 1 muffin tray, lightly oiled
What you do:	Fully preheat oven to 230°C/450°F/regulo 8.

Sponge the yeast in 150 ml/5 fl oz of tepid water with the teaspoon of treacle, leave in a warm place for the yeast to become active, about 5 minutes.

In a large, wide mixing bowl combine the flour with the salt. Make a well in the centre.

Add in the remaining water to the yeast and treacle mixture, stir well together. Pour into the dry ingredients and mix with an open hand, drawing the flour from the sides of the bowl.

Mix to a wettish dough, too wet to knead. Divide equally into the muffin tray.

Put the tray in a warm place, covered with a tea-towel. Leave for about 20 minutes. The buns will have risen to twice their original size.

Remove the tea-towel. Bake for 25–30 minutes, or until they look nicely browned and sound hollow when tapped.

Alternatively, you can remove the buns from the tins about 10 minutes before the end of cooking and put them back into the oven to crisp all round.

Ballymaloe White Yeast Bread

This loaf is always served in a traditional plait shape in Ballymaloe, but it can be shaped into many different forms, rolls, loaves, or even animal shapes! It is a traditional white yeast bread and, once you have mastered this basic technique, the sky is the limit. Keep an eye on the watch points listed at the start of this chapter.

Makes:	2 loaves or buns or plaits, quantity depending on size
Cooking time:	25–35 minutes
What you need:	• 20 g/$\frac{3}{4}$ oz fresh yeast
	• 425 ml/15 fl oz warm water
	• 680 g/1$\frac{1}{2}$ lb strong white flour
	• 2 teaspoons salt
	• 15 g/$\frac{1}{2}$ oz sugar
	• 25 g/1 oz butter
	• poppy seeds or sesame seeds for topping, optional
	• 2 loaf tins, 13 x 20 cm/ 5 x 8 in; or a baking sheet for plaits or buns
What you do:	Preheat your oven to 230°C/450°F/regulo 8.
	Sponge the yeast in 150 ml/5 fl oz of tepid water, leave in a warm place for about 5 minutes.

Into a large, wide mixing bowl, sieve the flour, salt and sugar. Rub in the butter, make a well in the centre.

Pour in the sponged yeast and most of the remaining lukewarm water. Mix to a loose dough, adding the remaining liquid or a little extra flour if needed.

Turn the dough onto a lightly floured work surface, cover and leave to relax for about 5 minutes.

Then knead for about 10 minutes or until smooth, springy and elastic. If kneading in a food mixer with a dough hook, 5 minutes is usually long enough.

Put the dough in a large ceramic bowl. Cover the top tightly with clingfilm to maintain the warm, moist atmosphere.

When the dough has more than doubled in size, after $1\frac{1}{2}$–2 hours, knock back and knead again for about 2–3 minutes. Leave to relax again for 10 minutes.

Divide and shape the dough into loaves, plaits or rolls, transfer to lightly oiled loaf tins or a baking sheet, as required, and cover with a light tea-towel. Allow to rise again in a warm place, until the shaped dough has again doubled in size.

The bread is ready for baking when a small dent remains if the dough is pressed lightly with the finger. Brush with egg wash and sprinkle with poppy or sesame seeds if you wish. Or dust lightly with flour for a rustic-looking loaf.

Bake for 25–35 minutes; exact time will depend on the size.

As always, when cooked, the bread will sound hollow when tapped. Cool on a wire rack.

To make a plait:
Take half the quantity of white yeast dough after it has been knocked back, divide into 3 equal pieces. With both hands, roll each one into a rope — the thickness depends on how fat you want the plait. Then pinch the 3 ends together at the top, bring each outside strand alternately into the centre to form a plait, pinch the ends and tuck in neatly. Transfer onto a baking tray. Allow to double in size. Egg wash or dredge with flour.

Easy Rye Bread with Caraway Seeds

A great bread for just about any occasion.

Makes:	1 loaf
Cooking time:	45–50 minutes

What you need:
- 310 g/11 oz strong white flour
- 150 g/5 oz rye flour
- 2–3 teaspoons caraway seeds
- 1 teaspoon salt
- 25 g/1 oz yeast
- 1 teaspoon treacle
- 450 ml/15 fl oz tepid water

What you do: Fully preheat oven to 230°C/450°F/regulo 8.

In a large, wide mixing bowl, combine the strong white flour, rye flour and caraway seeds, add the salt.

Sponge the yeast in 150 ml/5 fl oz of tepid water with the teaspoon of treacle, leave in a warm place for the yeast to become active, about 5 minutes.

Add the remaining water to the yeast and treacle mixture, then stir well. Pour into the dry ingredients and mix with an open hand, drawing the flour from the sides of the bowl.

Mix to a wettish dough. This dough will be too wet to knead. Pour into the lightly oiled loaf tin.

Put the tin in a warm place, cover with a tea-towel. Leave for about 30–40 minutes. The bread should double in size.

Remove the tea-towel. Bake for about 45–50 minutes, or until the bread looks nicely browned and sounds hollow when tapped.

Butter and Milk Clusters

This bread has a wonderfully soft texture. I love to make the dough into rolls and then bake them in a round tin, hence the 'cluster' in the name. When it's cooked it can be pulled apart.

Makes: 1 loaf

Cooking time: 45 minutes, approximately

What you need:
- 20 g/$\frac{3}{4}$ oz fresh yeast
- 425 ml/15 fl oz warm milk
- 680 g/1$\frac{1}{2}$ lb s strong white flour
- 50 g/2 oz butter
- 2 teaspoons salt
- 15 g/$\frac{1}{2}$ oz sugar
- poppy seeds or sesame seeds for topping, optional

What you do: Preheat the oven to 230°C/450°F/regulo 8.

Sponge the yeast in 150 ml/5 fl oz of tepid milk, leave in a warm place for about 5 minutes.

Sieve the flour, salt and sugar into a large, wide mixing bowl. Rub in the butter, then make a well in the centre. Pour in the sponged yeast and most of the remaining lukewarm milk. Mix to a loose dough, adding the remaining liquid or a little extra flour if needed.

Turn the dough onto a lightly floured work surface, cover and leave to relax for about 5 minutes.

Then knead for 10 minutes or until smooth, springy and elastic. If using a food mixer with a dough hook, 5 minutes should be long enough.

Put the dough in a large ceramic bowl. Cover the top tightly with clingfilm.

When the dough has more than doubled in size, after 1$\frac{1}{2}$–2 hours, knock back and knead again for about 2–3 minutes. Leave to relax again for 10 minutes.

Divide the dough and shape into rolls, transfer to the oiled tin and cover with a light tea-towel. Leave the dough in a warm place to rise again to double in size.

Test for when the dough is ready for baking by pressing the top lightly with your finger. A small dent should remain.

Brush with egg wash. Sprinkle with seeds if desired. Bake the bread for 45 minutes.

The cluster is ready when it looks golden brown. It may be necessary to remove this bread from the tin about three-quarters of the way through baking time to crisp up the bottom properly. Tap the bread and listen for the hollow sound that tells you it is cooked.

Cool the bread on a wire tray.

Breadsticks

These fun crunchy nibbles are great for having with drinks. You can be as creative as you want with the flavourings you use. Let you imagination run wild.

Makes: about 10

Cooking time: 8–15 minutes

What you need:
- 285 g/10 oz Garden Café pizza dough (see page 66), well-chilled
- coarse sea salt
- cumin seeds; sesame seeds; black pepper, coarsely ground; rosemary, freshly chopped; or any other herb or spice, according to preference

What you do: Preheat the oven to 220°C/425°F/regulo 7.

Once you have reached the stage where the dough has been proved, knock it back down and roll it into a rectangle about 22 x 1 cm/9 x $\frac{1}{2}$ in. Cut the dough into 1 cm/$\frac{1}{2}$ in strips.

Sprinkle the work surface with sea salt and your choice of flavouring.

Lay one strip of dough on top of your chosen 'sprinkle'. Put one hand at each end of the strip. Simultaneously slide one hand forward and the other backwards to twist the strip and coat it with salt, seeds or herbs.

Alternatively, just pull off small pieces of dough about 25 g/1 oz each, form into thin, medium or fat strips and then roll each one in the 'sprinkle'.

Repeat this process with all the breadsticks, placing each one on a lightly floured baking sheet. Bake for 8–15 minutes, depending on size, until golden brown and crisp. Cool on a wire rack.

Note:
Breadsticks are usually baked without a final rising but for a slightly, lighter result let the shaped dough rise for about 10 minutes before baking.

Carta Musica

Traditional Sardinian Flat Bread that is stunning to look at, and irresistible. It's great with roasted vegetables or just to serve with pre-dinner drinks. The beauty of this recipe is that it is so quick and easy, using this fast-acting yeast does away with the first rising.

Makes: 20–24

Cooking time: 5–10 minutes

What you need:
- 680 g/1$\frac{1}{2}$ lb strong white flour
- 1 packet fast-acting yeast
- 2 level teaspoons salt
- 15 g/$\frac{1}{2}$ oz sugar
- 2–4 tablespoons olive oil
- 350–400 ml/12–14 fl oz warm water, more if needed
- olive oil
- herbs, according to preference; singly, for example, rosemary, sage, thyme or marjoram; or a mixture
- sea salt

What you do: Preheat the oven to 230°C/450°F/regulo 8.

In a large, wide mixing bowl, sieve the flour and add the salt, sugar and fast-acting yeast. Mix all the ingredients thoroughly.

Make a well in the centre of the dry ingredients, add the oil and most of the water. Mix to a loose dough. Add more water or flour as necessary.

Turn out the dough onto a floured work surface, cover and leave to relax for about 5 minutes.

Then knead the dough for about 10 minutes or until smooth and springy. if kneading in a food mixer with a dough hook, 5 minutes will be long enough.

If you have time, it is a great advantage if you chill the dough at this point. It will make it easier to handle. Otherwise, leave the dough to relax again for about 10 minutes.

Heat a baking tray in the oven in advance.

Divide the dough into 20–24 pieces. Keep the dough and the individual pieces covered while you work. If you do not want to make so many in one sitting, the dough freezes perfectly well at this stage.

Roll out as thinly as possible into large paper-thin squares or rectangles. In fact, you can form any shape you like. Sometimes it is fun to cut it like fingers. It will shrink back, so roll out, leave to rest for a minute or so while you start to roll out 2 or 3 more, then return to the first and roll again, even more thinly this time. Or alternatively cut the dough into large triangles, squares or strips.

Brush the thin dough lightly with olive oil, sprinkle with chopped rosemary or your preferred herb or a mixture of freshly chopped herbs. Sprinkle with sea salt.

Slap onto the hot baking sheet and cook for 5–10 minutes. The bread will be bubbly and crisp. They look delicious!

Cool on a wire rack.

Granary Loaf

Granary flour is a mixture of malted wheat and rye, with a proportion of whole wheat kernels. Some people find the malt flavour rather strong, so you can mix a proportion of plain or strong white flour with the granary meal. Home-made granary bread stays fresh and moist for an unusually long time.

Makes:	1 loaf
Cooking time:	40 minutes, approximately
What you need:	• 450 g/1 lb granary flour
	• 110 g/4 oz strong white flour
	• 1 rounded teaspoon salt
	• 50 g/2 oz butter
	• 20 g/$\frac{3}{4}$ oz yeast
	• 1 teaspoon treacle, optional
	• 2 tablespoons olive oil
	• 300 ml/10 fl oz warm water, approximately
	• 25 g/1 oz kibbled wheat
	• 1 loaf tin, 13 x 20 cm/5 x 8 in

What you do: Preheat the oven to 230°C/450°F/regulo 8.

In a large, wide mixing bowl, combine the flour together with the salt and rub in the butter.

Mix the yeast with the water, treacle and oil.

Add the liquid to the flour and mix to a dough, which should be very soft, light and pliable.

Turn out onto a lightly floured work surface and knead for a few minutes. Cover and leave to rest.

Knead for a further 10 minutes, then form it into a ball. Put the dough in a large ceramic bowl. Cover the top tightly with clingfilm.

When the dough has at least doubled in bulk and is nice and puffy, this should take about $1\frac{1}{2}$–2 hours, knock it back and knead it for 2–3 minutes.

Put the dough into a well-oiled loaf tin, cover it with a clean tea-towel, leave to rise for a further 30–60 minutes, depending on the warmth of your kitchen and the moisture in the air. The dough will rise well above the rim.

Brush lightly with water and sprinkle with kibbled wheat.

Bake for 25 minutes, then reduce the heat to 200°C/400°F/regulo 6 for the remainder of the time, a further 20 minutes, approximately.

If you wish, you can remove the bread from the tin about 10 minutes before the end of cooking and put it back into the oven to crisp up all round. When the bread is fully baked, it will sound hollow when tapped.

Allow to cool on a wire rack.

Gluten-Free White Yeast Bread

Rosemary Kearney showed me how to make this wonderful bread. She came to the school first as a student, then stayed on to teach. She is herself a coeliac so understands only too well how difficult it can be to find delicious, tasty, gluten-free bread.

Makes: 1 loaf

Cooking time: 50–60 minutes

What you need:
- 250 g/9 oz rice flour
- 110 g/4 oz fine cornmeal
- $2\frac{1}{2}$ teaspoons Xantham gum
- $1\frac{1}{2}$ teaspoons salt
- 50 g/2 oz dried milk powder
- 85 g/3 oz caster sugar
- 5 teaspoons dried yeast powder
- 3 free-range eggs, medium-sized
- 300 ml/10 fl oz warm water
- 1 teaspoon white wine vinegar
- 900 g/2 lb loaf tin

What you do: Preheat the oven to 190°C/375°F/regulo 5.

In a large mixing bowl, combine all the dry ingredients and mix well together. Gluten-free flours are very fine and need to be very well blended before any liquid is added.

Whisk the eggs, add the water, and white wine vinegar and mix well.

Gradually add the liquid to the dry ingredients and beat well for approximately 10 minutes, preferably using an electric mixer. The consistency of the mixture is too wet to knead by hand.

Spoon the mixture into a well-oiled 2 lb loaf tin and cover with a clean tea-towel.

Allow the dough to rise to just over the level of the tin. Bake for 45 minutes. Remove from the tin and bake for a further 5–10 minutes until the bread sounds hollow when tapped.

Introduction to
Sweet Bread

This I suppose is one of the more indulgent chapters in the book. Almost everyone has a sweet tooth. Many will deny it, but in truth most of us mere mortals love something sweet once in a while. Somehow eating a sweet bread can ease the guilt a little. Not that we should feel any guilt at all.

Here I cover recipes ranging from a traditional tea brack to a vanilla bread. I have included recipes for my own versions of the classic French croissants and brioches, and also a delicious pecan brioche.

When taking the time and trouble to bake any bread, especially a sweet bread, the quality of the ingredients is critical. Things that often can really affect the end result are as simple as checking the hazelnuts or pecans are fresh and have not gone rancid or stale. Taste one or two before using them. When using chocolate check that the cocoa butter content is high; I recommend at least 50 per cent. This is what will give you the ultimate chocolate bread. Grind spices like cinnamon, cumin, cardamom fresh as and when you need them.

Some of you may notice I use salted butter in my croissants and brioches. This is bound to cause a little controversy as traditional French baking always calls for unsalted butter. I am Irish and have grown up in Ireland. I adore the taste of salted butter. For me using salted butter in my croissants adds an important dimension to the flavour. I can already hear the objections coming from classic French cooks around the world, friends and foe alike.

Croissants

These are the French breakfast pastry that we all know and love so well. Although this recipe may be daunting because of its length, it is worth the effort and time. Croissants are not hard to make, they just require lengthy resting times between stages. Start them the day before you want them so that you can serve coffee and fresh croissants the following morning. If you have a special somebody who you want to impress, home-baked croissants are the *grand prix* of morning treats.

Served with your own home-made strawberry jam (see page 141) or any filling you choose. Have fun!

Makes: 16 croissants

Cooking time: 20 minutes, approximately

What you need:
- 150 ml/5 fl oz milk
- 25 g/1 oz sugar
- 150 ml/5 fl oz water
- 25 g/1 oz yeast
- 450 g/1 lb strong white flour
- pinch of salt
- 285 g/10 oz butter

What you do: In a heavy-bottomed saucepan, heat the milk and dissolve the sugar in it, add the water and make sure all the liquid is tepid before pouring it onto the yeast. Stir until dissolved.

Into a large, wide mixing bowl, sieve the flour and add a pinch of salt. Rub 50 g/2 oz of the butter into the flour. Make a well in the centre.

Add the yeast liquid and mix to a soft dough. Knead until smooth, by hand or in a food mixer with a dough hook — about 8–10 minutes by hand or 5 minutes in a machine.

Cover with clingfilm and leave in the fridge for 2 hours.

Beat the remaining butter into a thin layer between sheets of clingfilm. Roll out the dough into a rectangle, put the butter on one half of the rectangle 2.5 cm/1 in from the edges all around and fold the other half over it.

Make sure your work surface is well floured, then flatten the dough with a rolling pin, and continue to roll out into a rectangle about

45.5 cm/18 inches long and 16 cm/6$\frac{1}{2}$ inches wide, don't worry if it doesn't measure exactly that size. Fold neatly into three with the sides as accurately aligned as possible. Seal the edges with a rolling pin.

Give the dough a quarter turn, 90 degrees, it should now be on your work surface as though it was a book with the open side facing right or left, it doesn't matter which. Roll out again, fold in three, again aligning the edges carefully, and seal the edges with the rolling pin. Cover with plastic wrap and rest the dough in the fridge for 30 minutes.

With the open ends facing right or left, roll out the pastry again, and fold in three as before. Cover and leave in the fridge until the next day.

Then turn the dough out onto a lightly floured work surface. Knock the air out of it. Roll and fold in three once again. If the room is very warm, you may need to chill your dough again before the final rolling and shaping.

Finally, roll out the dough to 5 mm/$\frac{1}{3}$ in thick, 33 cm/14 in wide and as long as possible, usually it will come out at about 56 cm/22 in. Trim the edges and cut into half lengthways and then into elongated triangles. The base of each should be about 15 cm/6 in, but you will have 2 smaller triangles at either end.

Preheat the oven to 220°C/425°F/regulo 7.

Start at the base of each triangle and roll it towards the tip. Pull the two into a half moon. Place the croissants on a baking sheet with the tip tucked underneath. Egg wash and put in a warm place to prove for 30–45 minutes or until they have doubled in size, then egg wash again very gently.

Bake in your fully preheated oven for 10 minutes then reduce the temperature to 180°C/350°F/regulo 4 and bake for 10 minutes more until the croissants are crisp and golden and brown on the bottom.

Delicious served with home-made strawberry jam, but croissants may be filled with all kinds of things. You choose!

Ballymaloe Brown Yeast Bread

Ballymaloe White Yeast Bread

Bread Sticks

Carta Musica

Brioche

Pecan Brioche

Lana Pringle's Tea Brack

Brioche

Brioche is the richest of all yeast doughs. It can often seem intimidating but this very easy version works well and this recipe has been designed so that the dough can rise overnight in the fridge and be shaped and baked the following morning.

My brother-in-law Eoin came on my bread course a few years ago and since then has had an open invitation to come for coffee and brioche every Sunday morning.

I always serve them warm from the oven with butter and home-made strawberry jam (see page 141).

Makes: 15–20 individual brioches

Cooking time: 20–25 minutes for individual brioches

What you need:
- 25 g/1 oz yeast
- 50 g/2 oz castor sugar
- 65 ml/2$\frac{1}{2}$ fl oz tepid water
- 4 eggs
- 450 g/1 lb strong white flour
- large pinch of salt
- 225 g/8 oz soft butter

- 15–20 individual moulds

Egg wash:
- 1–2 eggs, beaten

What you do: In the bowl of an electric mixer, sponge together the yeast and sugar in the tepid water. Allow to stand for 5 minutes. Add the eggs, flour and salt and mix to a stiff dough with the dough hook.

When the mixture is smooth, add the soft butter in small pieces and beat it in. Only add the next piece of butter when the previous piece has been completely absorbed. This kneading stage should take about 30 minutes.

The finished dough should have a silky appearance and should come away from the sides of the bowl. When you touch the dough, it should be damp but not sticky.

Place it in an oiled bowl, cover and rest it overnight in the fridge. The next day, prepare your brioche moulds.

Then, working quickly, remove the dough from the fridge, knock it back by folding it in on itself. It is crucial that you work quickly while the dough is still cool, otherwise the butter will begin to melt and the dough will become too sticky to handle.

Weigh the dough into 50 g/2 oz pieces and roll into balls. With the side of your hand roll each ball of dough into a teardrop shape, do this by rolling with the pressure slightly off centre. Put the dough heavy end first into the well-buttered brioche moulds. Push the 'little hat' towards the centre, leaving it just protruding above the body of the dough. Dip the thick end of a chop stick in a little flour and push it down through the dough almost to the bottom, this may sound strange but I have found it is the best method to keep the 'little hat' in place. Brush the top of each brioche gently with egg wash.

Allow them to prove in a warm place for 45 minutes to 1 hour until they have doubled in size. While they are rising, preheat the oven to 180°C/350°F/regulo 4. Egg wash the brioches very gently again. Cook for 20–25 minutes. Large brioches will take around 40–50 minutes to cook. You can tell they are cooked by inserting a skewer into the centre — it should come out clean.

Serve freshly baked with butter and home-made strawberry jam.

Pecan Brioche

What a gem of a recipe. Making brioches is something of a family passion. I have often been heard to say, 'If you really love someone, you will make them brioche.' Although this recipe is very different to my regular brioche recipe, it is equally good, and quickly became a firm favourite with my family and friends. It looks wonderful when sliced, with its double swirls of pecan in the rich dough. A real indulgence.

Makes:	1 loaf
Cooking time:	40–45 minutes
What you need:	• 625 g/1 lb 6 oz strong white flour
	• 1 orange, grated zest
	• 25 g/1 oz yeast
	• 50 g/2 oz sugar
	• 2 teaspoons salt
	• 125 ml/4 fl oz water
	• 6 eggs
	• 225 g/8 oz butter

Pecan paste:
• 50 g/2 oz butter
• 140 g/5 oz light brown sugar
• 1 egg
• 1 teaspoon vanilla extract
• 225 g/8 oz pecan nuts, finely chopped
• 25 g/1 oz butter

What you do: In the bowl of an electric mixer mix together 200 g/7 oz flour, the orange zest, yeast and sugar. Add the hot water and beat at a medium speed for 2 minutes.

Add the eggs, one at a time, beating well after each addition.

Gradually beat in a further 310 g/11 oz flour and the salt. When the mixture is completely blended, add the soft butter, a few pieces at a time.

When all the butter is added, reduce the speed and beat in the remaining 110 g/4 oz flour. When all the flour has been added continue to beat until the dough comes away from the sides of the bowl. When you touch the dough it should be damp but not sticky.

Put the dough into a well-oiled, deep bowl. Cover tightly with clingfilm and leave to rise in a cool place until it has doubled in size. This will take about 3 hours.

Knock the dough back down and cover again. Refrigerate for between 12 and 24 hours. Overnight is ideal.

To make the pecan paste, cream together the butter and brown sugar. Add the egg and beat until smooth. Add in the vanilla extract and pecan nuts. Set aside.

Oil two loaf tins. Turn the dough onto a lightly floured work surface. Divide the dough into 2 equal pieces. Roll each piece into a rectangle about 30.5 x 20.5 cm/12 x 8 in. Spread the pecan paste evenly over the rectangle. Leave a 2.5 cm/1 in border all the way round.

Starting along one of the long sides, roll the dough tightly about 15 cm/6 in towards the centre. Then roll from the other long side, 15 cm/6 in into the centre. Each side should be even in height and thickness. Turn the loaves over and put them into the oiled loaf tins with the seam side down.

Lightly brush the top of each loaf with melted butter. Cover with clingfilm and leave to rise until doubled in size, about 2–3 hours.

Preheat the oven to 180°C/350°F/regulo 4. Remove the clingfilm and bake in the centre of the oven for 40–45 minutes. The loaves will be golden brown and firm to the touch when fully cooked. Leave to cool in the tins for 10 minutes and then remove from the tins to cool further on a wire rack.

Elizabeth Mosse's Gingerbread

A classic gingerbread recipe, it is rich and moist. It brings back many fond memories of afternoon tea in front of the fire in Bennetsbridge. This gingerbread improves in flavour over time so it is an ideal store-cupboard recipe.

Makes: 2 loaves

Cooking time: 1 hour, approximately

What you need:
- 450 g/1 lb flour
- 1 teaspoons salt
- 1–2 teaspoons ground ginger
- 2 teaspoons baking powder
- 1 teaspoon bread soda, finely sieved
- 1 handful of sultanas
- 225 g/8 oz soft brown sugar
- 170 g/6 oz butter, cut into cubes
- 340 g/12 oz treacle
- 300 ml/12 fl oz milk
- 1 egg

- 2 loaf tins, lined

What you do: Preheat the oven to 180°C/350°F/regulo 4.

In a large wide bowl sieve all the dry ingredients together. In a saucepan gently warm the brown sugar with the cubed butter and treacle. Then add the milk. Allow the liquid to cool a little.

Make a well in the centre of the dry ingredients and stir in the liquid mixture. Add the beaten egg and the sultanas.

Mix very thoroughly and make sure that there are no little lumps of flour left. Bake in the loaf tins for 1 hour in the fully preheated oven.

It is vital that the oven door is not opened during cooking or the gingerbread will collapse.

Banana Bread

I have always loved this moist, tasty, banana bread. It keeps for up to two weeks in a tin but I doubt if you will get the chance to find out, as it will be gobbled up very quickly.

Makes: 1 large loaf

Cooking time: $1\frac{1}{2}$ hours, approximately

What you need:
- 225 g/8 oz self-raising flour
- $\frac{1}{2}$ level teaspoon salt
- 110 g/4 oz butter
- 170 g/6 oz castor sugar
- 110 g/4 oz sultanas or seedless raisins
- 25 g/1 oz chopped walnuts
- 110 g/4 oz cherries, washed and halved
- 2 eggs, preferably free-range
- 450 g/1 lb very ripe bananas, weighed without skins

- 1 loaf tin, 24 x 13.5 x 5 cm/$9\frac{1}{2}$ x $5\frac{1}{2}$ x 2 in, lined with greaseproof or silicone paper.

What you do: Preheat the oven to 180°C/350°F/regulo 4.

Into a large, wide mixing bowl, sieve the flour and salt. Rub in the butter, add the sugar. Stir in sultanas or seedless raisins, the walnuts and the glacé cherries. Mash the bananas with a fork, add the eggs and mix this well into the other ingredients.

The dough should have a nice soft consistency.

Pour the mixture into the lined tin and spread evenly. Place in the centre of your oven and bake for $1\frac{1}{2}$ hours. It is vital that the oven door is not opened during cooking or the banana bread will collapse.

Cool before removing from the tin.

Served thickly sliced, spread with soft butter, it's an ideal accompaniment to an afternoon cup of tea.

Cinnamon Swirl

This is a wonderful sweet bread, especially if you are a cinnamon lover. When I make this bread, the scent of warm bread mixed with spice always entices people towards my kitchen. It is a battle to keep the bread long enough to let it cool. I serve this bread sliced thickly. If by some miracle you have some left the next morning, Cinnamon Swirl is great toasted.

Makes: 2 loaves

Cooking time: 50 minutes, approximately

What you need:
- 25 g/1 oz fresh yeast
- 63 ml/$2\frac{1}{2}$ fl oz warm water
- pinch of granulated sugar
- 250 ml/8 fl oz warm milk
- 250 ml/8 fl oz warm water
- 70 g/$2\frac{1}{2}$ oz unsalted butter, melted
- 110 g/4 oz granulated sugar
- pinch of salt
- 2 eggs
- 1.185 kg/2 lb 10 oz strong flour

- 2 loaf tins

Cinnamon filling:
- 155 g/$5\frac{1}{2}$ oz light brown sugar
- 2 tablespoons ground cinnamon
- 25 g/1 oz unsalted butter

What you do: Into a small bowl, crumble the yeast into 63 ml/$2\frac{1}{2}$ fl oz of warm water, sprinkle on a pinch of granulated sugar and leave to sponge together for about 5 minutes.

In the bowl of an electric mixer, combine the rest of the water, milk, melted butter, sugar, salt, eggs and 285 g/10 oz flour and beat together for 1 minute. It will be a very wet dough at this point.

Stir the sponged yeast into the ingredients in the mixer. Add the rest of the flour 1 tablespoon at a time. Beat for a few minutes until it a soft dough is formed.

Turn out onto a lightly floured work surface and knead for about 5 minutes or until the dough is smooth and shiny.

Lightly oil a large. deep bowl, put in the dough and turn it over so that it gets coated with the oil. Cover with clingfilm and leave to rise in a warm place for about 2 hours or until doubled in size.

In a small bowl, mix the freshly ground cinnamon and light brown sugar. Set aside.

When the dough has risen fully turn out onto a floured work surface and knock it back down. Resist the temptation to work the dough any further, just divide it into 2 equal portions.

Roll each portion of the dough into a rectangle 23 x 30.5 cm/9 x 12 in. Brush each piece with melted butter and sprinkle evenly with cinnamon sugar. Leave a 2.5 cm/1 in border on all sides.

Keep back 1–2 tablespoons of cinnamon sugar for dusting the top of the bread.

Begin at the narrowest edge of the dough and gently roll it up like you would a Swiss roll. Pinch well along the edges and at both ends to seal in the sugar while it is baking.

Put the dough into the lightly oiled loaf tins with the seam side down. Brush the tops with melted butter and dust with the reserved cinnamon sugar. Cover loosely with clingfilm and leave to rise until it has doubled in size.

Bake in the centre of a preheated oven for 40 minutes. Remove from the tins and put straight back in the oven for a further 10 minutes.

Leave to cool a little on a wire rack. This bread is excellent eaten slightly warm.

Lana Pringle's Tea Brack

Lana, an old family friend, bakes these wonderful tea bracks. She has very kindly allowed me to use her recipe in this book. It keeps wonderfully well in a tin and is traditionally served sliced and buttered.

Makes: 2 loaves

Cooking time: 40–50 minutes

What you need:
- 400 g/14 oz dried fruit, raisins and sultanas
- 425 ml/15 fl oz tea
- 50 g/2 oz glacé cherries
- 50 g/2 oz chopped candied peel
- 110 g/4 oz soft brown sugar
- 110 g/4 oz granulated sugar
- 1 egg
- 400 g/14 oz plain white flour
- 1 teaspoon of baking powder

- 2 loaf tins lined with baking parchment

What you do: Fully preheat your oven to 180°C/350°F/regulo 4.

Put the raisins and sultanas into a bowl, cover with good quality strong tea and leave overnight to allow the fruit to plump up nicely.

Next day, add the halved cherries, chopped candied peel, sugar and egg and mix well. Sieve the flour and baking powder and stir in thoroughly. The mixture should be softish, so add a little more tea if necessary.

Divide the mixture between the two lined tins and bake in your fully preheated oven for 40–50 minutes until a skewer comes out clean.

Chocolate and Nut Bread

This is not too sweet a bread despite being chocolate, and it is great eaten with soft butter, cream cheese or even chocolate butter! (See page 142 for how to make this yummy addition to your repertoire.) This bread is really fast to make and children of all ages will adore it.

Makes:	2 loaves
Cooking time:	45 minutes, approximately

What you need:
- 85 g/3 oz unsweetened chocolate
- 110 g/4 oz soft butter
- 450 g/1 lb plain flour
- 1 teaspoon baking powder
- 1 level teaspoon of bread soda, finely sieved
- 1 teaspoon salt
- 225 g/8 oz castor sugar
- 2 eggs
- 200 ml/7 fl oz milk
- 2 teaspoons pure vanilla extract
- 70 g/$2\frac{1}{2}$ oz chopped hazel nuts

- 2 loaf tins, oiled

What you do: Fully preheat the oven to 180°C/350°F/regulo 4.

Bring a saucepan half-filled with water to the boil, put a Pyrex bowl over the pan of water, and make sure the base of the bowl does not touch the water. Turn off the heat under the saucepan. Leave the chocolate to melt in the bowl. Stir in the soft butter and set aside.

In a large, wide mixing bowl, combine the flour, baking powder, bread soda and salt.

In another mixing bowl, beat together the sugar, eggs, milk, vanilla and chopped nuts.

Bring the dry ingredients into this mixture. Add the chocolate mixture and beat until the batter is smooth.

Divide the mixture evenly between the 2 prepared loaf tins. Cook for 45 minutes or until a skewer inserted into the centre comes out clean. Remove from the oven and let the loaves cool in the tins for 5 minutes. Then turn out onto a wire rack until completely cold.

Dodo's Stollen

This recipe for Stollen was given to me by Dodo, Rachel's brother-in-law. It is a family recipe of Dodo's. Stollen is a traditional German Christmas cake. Don't be put off by the amount of ingredients, it is not a difficult recipe. Although it can be eaten on the day it's made, Dodo recommends keeping it a week in an airtight container so the flavours mature. Stollen also freezes very well.

Makes: 2 loaves

Cooking time: 40–45 minutes

What you need:
- 140 g/5 oz raisins
- 50 g/2 oz sultans
- 100 g/$3\frac{1}{2}$ oz currants
- 100 g/$3\frac{1}{2}$ oz candied peel
- 100 g/$3\frac{1}{2}$ oz almonds, blanched
- $\frac{1}{2}$ teaspoon vanilla extract
- 50 ml/2 fl oz Jamaican rum
- 225 ml/8 fl oz warm milk
- 25 g/1 oz yeast
- 500 g/1 lb 2 oz strong white flour
- pinch of salt
- 1–2 teaspoons ground coriander seeds
- $\frac{1}{2}$ teaspoon ground cardamom
- $\frac{1}{3}$ teaspoon grated nutmeg
- pinch of freshly ground black pepper
- 2 lemons, grated zest
- 100 g/$3\frac{1}{2}$ oz sugar
- 140 g/5 oz butter
- 225 g/8 oz marzipan (see page 142)
- icing sugar for dusting

What you do: In a large, wide mixing bowl place all the dried fruit together with the rum, almonds and vanilla. Cover and leave to soak while you make the dough.

Sponge the yeast in a bowl with the warm milk. Leave aside for about 5 minutes.

Mix the flour, salt, spices and lemon zest together and make a well in the centre. Pour in the sponged yeast mixture. Using your hand or a wooden spoon, draw enough of the flour into the yeast mixture to form a soft dough. Cover with a tea towel and leave to relax for 10 minutes.

Add the sugar and soft butter in the centre of the dough. Turn out onto a lightly floured work surface and knead until smooth. Kneading the butter and sugar in can be really messy, if you want you can use a food mixer with a dough hook. It takes approximately 10 minutes kneading by hand. The dough should be smooth and elastic.

Put the dough into an oiled bowl and leave to rest for about 2 hours or until the dough has doubled in size.

Knock back, turn the dough onto a lightly floured work surface and leave to rest for a further 10 minutes.

Flatten the dough out with your hands into a square, about 2.5 cm/1 in thick.

Scatter the soaked fruits evenly over the surface. Knead the dough again, being careful to incorporate all the fruits evenly. This is where it gets messy again!

Divide the dough into 2 equal pieces and roll out to about 15 x 20.5 cm/ 6 x 8 in and about 2.5 cm/1 in high. Divide the marzipan into 2 equal pieces of 110 g/4 oz each. Roll each piece of marzipan to form a sausage shape just less than the length of the dough.

Take one piece of dough and place the marzipan lengthways across the centre of the dough, leaving a little space at each end. Carefully fold the dough over the marzipan and place the whole thing seam side down onto a baking sheet. Repeat with the second piece of dough.

Remember to leave lots of room on the baking sheets as the Stollen will expand as it proves. Cover and leave to rise for about 1 hour, until it has doubled in size.

Bake in the fully preheated oven for 40–45 minutes or until fully cooked. Leave to cool completely.

Dust generously with icing sugar before serving.

Shortbread

Many memories are associated with the Aga that dominates our kitchen in Kinoith. When the children were small, it was where we hid the shortbread. But, children being children, they soon found the hiding place, as did all of our friends. We always have a tray of these buttery delights in the coolest oven of the 4-door Aga (where they keep that just-baked crispness). Our youngest daughter Emily loves to spread the top of the biscuits with home-made strawberry jam (see page 141), but most of us just enjoy them with a cup of tea. They are very quick and easy to make.

Makes: 24–32, depending on size

Cooking time: 20–30 minutes

What you need:
- 340 g/12 oz plain white flour
- 285 g/10 oz butter, well-chilled
- 110 g/4 oz castor sugar
- 85 g/3 oz ground rice
- good pinch of salt
- good pinch of baking powder
- castor sugar for sprinkling

- 1 Swiss roll tin, 25.5 x 38 cm/10 x 15 in

What you do: Preheat oven to 180°C/350°F/regulo 4.

Put all the dry ingredients into the bowl of a food processor. Cut the cold butter into cubes and add to the dry ingredients. Whiz the whole lot together in the food processor till it resembles fine breadcrumbs.

Spread the mixture evenly into your tin. Take a piece of clingfilm a little longer than the tin and place over the top. Depending on the width of your clingfilm you may need to use two sheets overlapping. Using a rolling pin and pressing through the clingfilm, make the dough flat, even and smooth.

Bake for 20–30 minutes. The shortbread should be a pale golden colour but fully cooked through. Cut into squares or fingers while still hot. Sprinkle with castor or vanilla sugar and allow to cool in the tin.

Store in an airtight container. If you have an Aga, the coolest oven is the ideal place to keep the shortbread, just don't tell anyone!

Vanilla Bread

This is a wonderful bread with a surprising vanilla flavour. I serve it sliced and spread with lashings of chocolate butter (page 142), or it's great with home-made raspberry jam (page 140).

Makes: 2 loaves

Cooking time: 45–50 minutes

What you need:
- 350 ml/12 fl oz milk
- 1 vanilla pod
- 25 g/1 oz yeast
- 1 tablespoon sugar
- 1 teaspoon salt
- 1–2 tablespoons vanilla extract
- 530 g/1 lb 3 oz strong white flour

What you do: Infuse the split vanilla pod in the milk for 10 minutes. Then heat the milk until it is tepid and pour it into a large mixing bowl on top of the yeast. Leave to sponge about 5 minutes.

Add the sugar, salt, vanilla extract and 4 tablespoons of the flour.

Beat briskly for 2 minutes. Add the rest of the flour to make a soft manageable dough.

Turn out onto a lightly floured work surface and knead for 2–3 minutes. Cover and leave to rest for 10 minutes.

Lightly dust the work surface with flour and start to knead the dough. When the dough becomes smooth and elastic put it in a lightly oiled bowl, cover and leave to rise for about 2 hours or until it has doubled in size.

Knock the dough back and turn it out onto a lightly floured work surface. Divide the dough into 2 pieces. Shape into free-form loaves — Vienna rolls — and place onto 2 lightly oiled baking sheets. Cover and leave to rise again for about 1 hour or until doubled in size.

Bake for about 45–50 minutes. When cooked, they will sound hollow when tapped.

Leave to cool fully on a wire rack.

Introduction to
Pizza and Focaccia

Pizza, the ultimate fast food, universally loved by all. Unfortunately due to our ever busier lifestyles and increasing time pressures, all too often it's a cardboard frozen pizza from the supermarket chill cabinet that is eaten in homes across the land. Or a lukewarm soggy pizza delivered to your door. These 'pizza's' bear little resemblance to the real thing.

I want to open up to you a world of home-made pizzas. In this chapter, we will discover how to make the bases, and how to use the delicious tomato sauces and toppings (see 'Essential Extras' for these). There are recipes for yeast bases, a gluten-free base and a superfast soda bread base. We will also take a look at that great Italian flat bread, focaccia, with some of its exciting variations.

In the cookery school we have a wood-burning pizza oven, a luxury most of you will not have. We built it 4 years ago, the pizzas cook in just 2 or 3 minutes. It is lit for our pizza workshops. Don't worry though, I have also been making pizza in a regular oven for many, many years and the results have always been successful!

When I serve pizza I like to eat it with a fresh green salad. This is one of the many marriages of flavour made in heaven. (See page 143 for my own Kinoith Summer Garden Salad, with a delicious honey-sweet dressing.)

It is important when making pizza or focaccia not to overdo the toppings. It is often tempting to pile on lots and lots of different things. Try to keep it simple, so that each flavour gets a chance to shine out. I think 4 or 5 different flavours on a pizza is plenty. Here are some of my very favourite pizza toppings and combinations:

- Smoked wild salmon, cream cheese, capers and chive flowers
- Ardsallagh soft goat's cheese, red onions, mozzarella and black olive tapenade
- Cashel blue cheese with caramelised onions and rosemary
- Roasted red onion, gruyère cheese and thyme leaves.

Garden Café Pizza Dough

The beauty of this recipe is that it is so quick and easy. Using this fast-acting yeast does away with the first rising. By the time your tomato sauce is bubbling in the oven your pizza base will be ready for its topping!

Makes: 8 pizza bases, 25.5 cm/10 in each approximately

What you need:
- 680 g/1$\frac{1}{2}$ lb s strong white flour
- 50 g/2 oz butter
- 1 packet fast-acting yeast
- 2 level teaspoons salt
- 15 g/$\frac{1}{2}$ oz sugar
- 2–4 tablespoons olive oil
- 350–400 ml/12–14 fl oz lukewarm water, more if needed

What you do: Into a large, wide mixing bowl, sieve the flour, add in the salt and sugar and rub in the butter. Stir in the fast-acting yeast and mix all the ingredients thoroughly.

Make a well in the centre of the dry ingredients, add the oil and most of the lukewarm water. Mix to a loose dough. You can add more water or flour if needed.

Turn the dough out onto a lightly floured work top, cover and leave to relax for about 5 minutes.

Then knead the dough for about 10 minutes or until smooth and springy. If kneading in a food mixer with a dough hook, 5 minutes is usually long enough.

Leave the dough to relax again for about 10 minutes. Shape and measure into 8 equal balls of dough each weighing approximately 140 g/5 oz. Lightly brush the balls of dough with olive oil.

If you have time, put the oiled balls of dough into a plastic bag and chill. The dough will be easier to handle when cold but it can be used immediately.

On a well-floured work surface, roll each ball out to a disc about 25.5 cm/10 in.

I find it convenient to pop a few rolled-out uncooked pizza bases into the freezer. You can take one out, put the topping on and slide it straight into the oven. What could be easier!

This dough also makes delicious white yeast bread which can be shaped into rolls, loaves and plaits.

Olive Oil Pizza Dough

This basic dough is ideal for pizza and focaccia. Try to use Italian extra virgin olive oil for a really authentic flavour.

Makes: 8 pizza bases, 25.5 cm/10 in each, approximately

What you need:
- 20 g/$\frac{3}{4}$ oz fresh yeast
- 225 ml/8 fl oz water
- 50 ml/2 fl oz olive oil
- 25 g/1 oz butter
- 1 teaspoon salt
- 15 g/$\frac{1}{2}$ oz sugar
- 450 g/1 lb strong white flour

What you do: Sponge the yeast in 150 ml/5 fl oz of tepid water, leave in a warm place for about five minutes.

Into a large, wide mixing bowl, sieve the flour, salt and sugar. Rub in the butter, make a well in the centre.

Pour in the sponged yeast, olive oil and most of the remaining lukewarm water. Mix to a loose dough adding the remaining liquid or a little extra flour if needed.

Turn the dough out onto a lightly floured work surface, cover and leave to relax for about 5 minutes.

Then knead by hand for about 10 minutes or until smooth, springy and elastic, or alternatively 5 minutes kneading in a food mixer with a dough hook will be long enough.

Put the dough in a large ceramic bowl. Cover the top tightly with clingfilm.

When the dough has more than doubled in size after about 1$\frac{1}{2}$–2 hours, knock back and knead again for about 2 to 3 minutes. Leave to relax again for 10 minutes.

On a well-floured work surface, roll out each ball to a round of about 25.5 cm/10 in and use as required.

Gluten-Free Pizza Base

Often when people discover they have a gluten intolerance they fear it could be very limiting. This does not have to be to the case. Here is a super, easy pizza base. Particularly good for kids' parties.

Makes:	4
Cooking time:	23–25 minutes

What you need:
- 170 g/6 oz rice flour
- 85 g/3 oz potato flour
- 50 g/2 oz tapioca
- 25 g/1 oz dried milk powder
- 1 teaspoon sugar
- 15 g/$\frac{1}{2}$ oz dried fast-acting yeast
- 40 g/1$\frac{1}{2}$ oz gluten-free baking powder
- 1 teaspoon xantham gum
- 1 teaspoon salt
- 1 tablespoon sunflower oil
- 1 egg
- 225 ml/8 fl oz lukewarm water

What you do: Preheat the oven to 190°C/375°F/regulo 5.

In a small bowl dissolve the sugar in the lukewarm water, sprinkle on the dried yeast.

In a large, wide mixing bowl mix together the rice flour, potato flour, tapioca, dried milk powder, baking powder, xanthan gum and salt.

Whisk the sunflower oil and eggs into the dry ingredients. Add in the yeast and sugar mixture. Combine well. Mix to a soft pliable dough.

Turn out onto a lightly floured work surface and divide into 4 equal pieces.

Cover a baking tray with baking parchment paper, dust with rice flour.

Gently shape each piece of dough into 20.5 cm/8 in circle. Leave the edges slightly higher.

Cover the dough with a tea towel and leave to rise for 15 minutes.

Bake the bases in the hot oven for 8–10 minutes. Then put on your chosen toppings and put back in the oven for 15 minutes.

Serve with a green salad.

Pizza Margherita

Possibly the most traditional and universally popular pizza in Italy. As this pizza is basically cheese and tomato, it is crucial your tomato sauce has a really super flavour.

Makes:	1, 25.5 cm/10 in pizza
Cooking time:	10–12 minutes
What you need:	• 140 g/5 oz pizza dough of your choice (see page 66 or 67) • 170 g/6 oz mozzarella cheese • 3 tablespoons olive oil • 4 tablespoons Isaac's Roasted Tomato Sauce (see page 144) • 1 tablespoon Parmesan (Parmigiano Reggiano is best), freshly grated • 1 dessertspoon annual marjoram, freshly chopped • semolina
What you do:	Preheat the oven to 250°C/475°F/regulo 9. Grate the mozzarella and sprinkle with the olive oil. Roll out the pizza dough or use a base you have previously prepared. Sprinkle a little semolina all over the surface of the pizza paddle and put the pizza base on top. If not using a pizza paddle, you can place the pizza dough directly onto a baking tray. Scatter the grated mozzarella over the base to within 2.5 cm/1 in of the edge. Spread Isaac's Roasted Tomato Sauce over the top. Sprinkle with the freshly grated Parmesan. Season very well with salt and freshly ground black pepper. Bake for 10–12 minutes or until the base is crisp and the top is bubbly and golden. Sprinkle the freshly chopped marjoram on top and serve immediately.

Cian's Garlic Pizza

A pizza for all you garlic addicts out there. Cian worked at the school last summer and developed this great pizza.

Makes:	1, 25.5 cm/10 in pizza
Cooking time:	10–12 minutes
What you need:	• 140 g/5 oz Garden Café pizza dough (see page 66)
	• 5 heaped teaspoons garlic butter (see page 144)
	• 85 g/3 oz gruyère cheese
	• garlic flowers and leaves when in season
	• parsley, freshly chopped
	• semolina
What you do:	Preheat the oven to 250°C/475°F/regulo 9.

Roll out the pizza dough or use a base you have prepared in advance. Sprinkle a little semolina all over the surface of the pizza paddle and put the pizza base on top, or alternatively, place the dough straight onto a baking tray.

Scatter the garlic butter in lumps over the top. Sprinkle the grated cheese. Season well with salt and freshly ground black pepper.

Bake in the fully preheated oven for 10–12 minutes or until the base is crisp and the top is bubbly and golden. Sprinkle the garlic flowers and leaves or the freshly chopped parsley on top, serve immediately, piping hot.

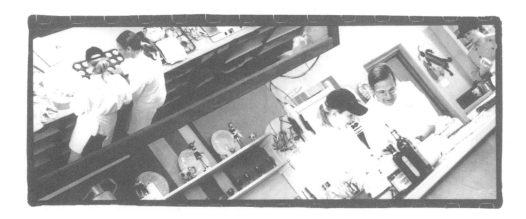

Calzone

Makes: 1 for a very hungry person, or serves 2 who feel sharing is fun!

Cooking time: 20–30 minutes

What you need:
- 140 g/5 oz fresh Garden Café pizza dough (see page 66), about one-sixth of the recipe
- semolina
- olive oil for brushing

Filling:
- 50 g/2 oz goat's cheese, crumbled
- 50 g/2 oz mozzarella cheese, roughly grated, soaked in 1 tablespoon of olive oil
- 1 teaspoon parsley, finely chopped
- 1 teaspoon annual marjoram, finely chopped
- 110 g/4 oz crispy bacon
- 2 tablespoons Piperonata (see page 145)

What you do: Preheat the oven to 250°C/475°F/regulo 9.

Soak the mozzarella in the olive oil for about 10 minutes. In a separate bowl, mix all the ingredients for the filling together. Set aside.

Roll out the dough very thinly into a 30 cm/12 in round. Sprinkle the pizza paddle, if using it, with semolina. Gently place the dough on top of the paddle. Otherwise a baking tray is fine. Just place the dough straight onto it.

Spoon the filling over half the disc to within about 2.5 cm/1 in of the edge.

Brush the edge with water, fold over the rest of the dough and seal by pinching the edge together with your fingers.

Brush the top with cold water and slide into the fully preheated oven.

Bake for 20–30 minutes. Brush with olive oil when baked and serve with a green salad.

Piadina Romagnola

Piadina Romagnola, often called pizza biscuits, are delicious spread with cream cheese mixed with fresh herbs, perhaps a slice of parma ham, smoked salmon or a few slices of very ripe tomato. Thin strips of roasted peppers also make a delicious topping either on their own or with cream cheese.

Makes:	about 10
Cooking time:	2–3 minutes each side
What you need:	• 15 g/$\frac{1}{2}$ oz fresh yeast • 1 generous teaspoon salt • 125 ml/4 fl oz milk, tepid • 125 ml/4 fl oz water, tepid • 1 teaspoon sugar • 450 g/1 lb strong white flour • 85 g/3 oz butter
What you do:	Mix the yeast with a little of the milk and water combined, gently stir in the sugar, leave in a warm place to sponge. Sieve the flour and salt into a large, wide bowl, rub in the butter. Mix the dissolved yeast with the remainder of the tepid liquid. Make a well in the centre of the flour and mix to a pliable dough. Knead the dough for a few minutes or until smooth. Cut the dough into small pieces 140 g/5 oz in weight. Roll out very thinly into discs 23 cm/9 in across, and not more than 5 mm/$\frac{1}{4}$ in thick. Preheat a griddle or heavy cast iron frying pan. Cook one piadini at a time, moving it every few seconds, so it doesn't stick. When it is brown and speckled on one side, turn it over and continue to cook on the other side. Eat warm or cold.

Timmy's Deep-Pan Pizza

This quick and easy pizza recipe is ideal for feeding a gang of hungry kids as it takes less than 40 minutes altogether. I started to make this pizza quite by accident when our 2 youngest were still in school. It was an easy way to get good healthy food into them fast. At the time Lydia was vegetarian and her younger sister Emily ate meat quite happily. To stop the rows and keep life peaceful, I would make one end vegetarian and put meat on the other. Everyone was happy!

Makes: 1 deep-pan pizza

Cooking time: 20–25 minutes

What you need:
- 450 g/1 lb White Soda Bread dough (page 2)
- 8 tablespoons Timmy's Tomato Fondue (see page 145)
- 4–6 slices garlic salami, chopped
- 6 button mushrooms, sliced
- 1 small red onion, finely sliced
- 2 tablespoons fresh parsley, annual marjoram and thyme, chopped
- 85 g/3 oz cheddar cheese, grated
- pepper and salt
- a selection of toppings of your choice
- 1 roasting tin, 35 x 30 cm/14 x 12 in, well-oiled

What you do: First, fully preheat your oven to 230°C/450°F/regulo 8.

Make the white soda bread dough in the usual way. Roll it out thinly to fit the roasting tin.

Spread a thin layer of the tomato fondue on the dough. Sprinkle on the chopped salami, sliced mushrooms and red onion. Scatter on the fresh herbs. Season very well with pepper and salt. Cover with grated cheese

Bake in your fully preheated oven for 20–25 minutes.

Serve immediately with a tasty green salad.

Focaccia

The classic Italian flat bread, great as a nibble before and during dinner.

Makes:	1 large focaccia, 25.5 x 30.5 cm/10 x 12 in; or 4 individual ones, 10 cm/6 in each
Cooking time:	20–25 minutes
What you need:	• 1 olive oil pizza dough (see page 67) • olive oil and sea salt
What you do:	Preheat the oven to 230°C/450°F/regulo 8. Roll out your dough, either into one large rectangle or four small discs. Whichever you choose, the dough needs to be about 1 cm/$\frac{1}{2}$ in thick. Place on an oiled baking sheet and make deep indentations all over the surface with your fingers. Brush liberally with olive oil and sprinkle with sea salt. Allow the dough to rise again. Then put it into oven and bake for 5 minutes, then reduce the temperature to 200°C/400°F/regulo 6 and bake for a further 15–20 minutes.

Focaccia with Rosemary

Another favourite is to sprinkle 2 teaspoons of finely chopped rosemary over the oil. Then sprinkle with sea salt and proceed and bake as above.

Focaccia with Sage

Knead 2 teaspoons of finely chopped sage into the piece of dough, then proceed, brushing on the olive oil and adding sea salt, proving one more time, then baking, as above.

Focaccia with Black Olives

Substitute 1–2 tablespoons of chopped black olives for the sage and proceed as above. Remember to take the stones out of the olives! 1 teaspoon of chopped marjoram or thyme leaves is a delicious addition here also.

Potato Focaccia

We tend to forget that Italian food often includes potatoes, so fixed are we on the idea of pasta being a staple in Italy. When I came across this gem of a combination of a focaccia dough made with potatoes and topped with sliced, cooked potatoes, I was hooked. It's great with a crunchy green salad at lunchtime or as part of a light, nourishing supper.

Makes: 2 focaccia

Cooking time: 15–20 minutes

What you need:
- 570 g/1$\frac{1}{4}$ lb, about 3, medium-sized potatoes
- water, to cook potatoes
- 63 ml/2$\frac{1}{2}$ fl oz olive oil
- 25 g/1 oz yeast
- 450 g/1 lb strong white flour
- 50 g/2 oz wholemeal flour
- 2 teaspoons salt
- $\frac{1}{2}$ teaspoon freshly ground black pepper
- 3 teaspoons thyme, chopped
- cornmeal, for dusting the baking sheet

What you do: Preheat the oven to 230°C/450°F/regulo 8.

Cook the potatoes and drain. Keep the cooking liquid and leave to cool. Measure 350 ml/12 fl oz of the liquid and put it in the bowl of an electric mixer. Add 50 ml/2 fl oz of the olive oil to it.

Sponge the yeast by sprinkling over the liquid in the mixer, leave for 2 minutes. Add the flour, salt, pepper and chopped thyme. Mix with the dough hook for approximately 10 minutes until the dough is silky and smooth.

Transfer the dough to a lightly oiled bowl, cover with clingfilm and leave to prove in a warm place for 1 hour or until the dough has doubled in size.

Keep one-third of the potatoes aside.

When the dough has risen knock it back and knead in two-thirds of the cooked potato until evenly distributed.

Put the dough back in the bowl and leave to rise for a further 30 minutes.

Turn the dough out onto a lightly floured work surface. Divide into 2 equal pieces. Gently pull and stretch each ball of dough until it is a circle approximately 23 cm/9 in across. Brush the tops with the remaining olive oil. Arrange the sliced potatoes on top. Sprinkle with sea salt.

Dust a baking sheet with cornmeal, put the focaccias onto the sheet, cover and leave in a warm place to rise for a further 15 minutes.

While the dough is rising, put a pizza stone or a baking sheet into the hot oven. Slide the focaccias onto the hot stone or baking sheet.

Bake in the fully preheated oven for 15–20 minutes or until the focaccias are golden brown.

Baked Dough Balls

A delightful and unusual starter or side dish. When we are having a 'pizza party' we often start by putting a tray of these dough balls into the oven, they cook in almost no time and are bound to cause a stir. Your guests can nibble on these as their pizzas cook.

Makes:	12–14 dough balls
Cooking time:	5–10 minutes
What you need:	• 140 g/5 oz Garden Café pizza dough (see page 66)
	• 2 teaspoons chives, freshly chopped
	• 2 teaspoons marjoram, freshly chopped
	• olive oil
	• garlic butter (see page 144), to serve
What you do:	Preheat the oven to 230°C/450°F/regulo 8.

Knead the finely chopped herbs into the piece of dough, then roll out to 1 cm/$\frac{1}{2}$ in thick. Cut the dough with a small, round 2 cm/$\frac{3}{4}$ in dough cutter.

Put the dough balls onto an oiled baking sheet and allow to rise again for about 10 minutes. Place in the oven and bake for 5–10 minutes.

Serve straight from the oven with a ramekin of garlic butter.

Garlic Pizza Bread

A novel way to make garlic bread, I use our pizza dough as the base, then when I take it out of the oven I smother it in garlic butter (see page 144). You'll never look at garlic bread the same way again.

Makes:	4 garlic pizza breads
Cooking time:	10–15 minutes
What you need:	• 285 g/10 oz Garden Café pizza dough (see page 66) • olive oil and sea salt • garlic butter, to taste (see page 144)
What you do:	Preheat the oven to 230°C/450°F/regulo 8.

Divide your dough into 4 and roll into roughly round shapes, about 1 cm/$\frac{1}{2}$ in thick.

Place on an oiled baking sheet. Brush liberally with olive oil and sprinkle with sea salt.

Allow the dough to rise again for about 10 minutes. With a sharp smooth-edged knife, slash each disc about 2–3 times across.

Bake for 10–15 minutes or until lightly browned. Remove from the oven and immediately brush liberally with garlic butter.

Introduction to
Sweet Buns

Everybody loves sweet things to munch on with their morning coffee or cup of afternoon tea. The buns in this chapter will be sure to make you very popular. As soon as you take any of the following sweet creations from your oven, the hordes will descend upon you like bears on a beehive.

I would go so far as to say that the satisfaction you will feel on removing any of these soft, sweet treats from the oven borders on childlike excitement. Then the bittersweet moment when the product of all your loving hard work is devoured by friends and family with such speed. Delight and appreciation will fill their eyes and sticky faces but you can feel a sort of loss that your beautiful buns have vanished and all that remains of your hard work is a few crumbs.

Each of the recipes I have chosen to show you is somebody's favourite. Your own will no doubt be included here too.

London Buns

My father, Ivan Allen, always loved a London bun with a cup of coffee. Whenever I make this recipe I think of him having a cup of coffee and a London bun in Thompson's Tivoli Café in Cork.

Makes:	18
Cooking time:	8–10 minutes
What you need:	• 450 g/1 lb baker's flour
	• pinch of salt
	• 85 g/3 oz castor sugar
	• 85 g/3 oz butter
	• 25 g/1 oz fresh yeast
	• 1 tablespoon castor sugar
	• 50 ml/2 fl oz warm water
	• 225–300 ml/8–10 fl oz warm water
	• 1 egg

Filling:
- 110 g/4 oz sultanas
- 50 g/2 oz candied peel
- 50 g/2 oz granulated sugar
- 1 lemon, grated zest
- egg wash

What you do: Heat the oven to 220°C/425°F/regulo 7.

In a large, wide mixing bowl, sieve in the flour and then add the salt and the 85 g/3 oz castor sugar. Rub in the butter. Mix well.

In a measuring jug dissolve the yeast with the tablespoon of sugar in the 50 ml/2 fl oz of tepid water.

In a bowl, whisk the egg and add the water, the water should be warm 'blood heat'. Pour this into the measuring jug with the yeast mixture.

Make a well in the centre of the dry ingredients. Pour in the liquid. Mix to a soft dough and add more liquid if necessary.

Turn the dough out onto a well-floured work surface, leave to rest for 5–10 minutes then knead until the dough is smooth and shiny.

Put the dough in a clean bowl, cover the bowl and let the dough rise in a warm place until it doubles in size.

When the dough has doubled in size, knock it back and leave to rest for a few minutes longer. Then turn out onto a well-floured work surface.

Knead the sultanas, peel, sugar and lemon zest into the bun dough. Roll the dough into a thick cylinder. Divide into 18 equal pieces, approximately 50 g/2 oz each. Roll into buns. Place them on a lightly floured baking sheet.

Flatten the buns very slightly and brush them with egg wash. Sprinkle with sugar. Cover loosely and allow to rise for about 45 minutes or until the buns have doubled in size.

Egg wash again and bake in your preheated oven for 8–10 minutes or until golden. Cool on a wire rack.

Barrack Buns

When I first made these buns at the school, they brought back memories to nearly everybody who tasted one. I heard stories about sitting in cafés on wet, winter days, gossiping and enjoying these cream buns. Rosalie Dunne, who has worked with us at the school almost since we started, told me that as a child growing up, her father would buy these buns on his way home from Collins' Barracks in Cork as a treat. To this day, Rosalie calls them 'Barrack Buns'. They are a real comfort food.

Makes: 18

Cooking time: 15 minutes approximately

What you need:
- 450 g/1 lb baker's flour
- pinch of salt
- 85 g/3 oz castor sugar
- 85 g/3 oz butter
- 25 g/1 oz fresh yeast
- 1 tablespoon castor sugar
- 225–300 ml/8–10 fl oz warm milk
- 1 egg

Filling:
- 225 ml/8 fl oz cream
- 3 tablespoons home-made raspberry jam (see page 140)
- icing sugar, for dusting

What you do: Fully preheat the oven to 220°C/425°F/regulo 7.

In a large, wide mixing bowl sieve in the flour, add the salt and the 85 g/3 oz castor sugar. Rub in the butter. Mix well.

In a measuring jug, dissolve the yeast with the tablespoon of castor sugar in 50 ml/2 fl oz of tepid milk.

Whisk the eggs and add the warm milk. Pour this into the measuring jug with the yeast mixture and stir well.

Make a well in the centre of the dry ingredients and add the egg, milk and yeast mixture. Mix to a soft dough, adding more milk if you need to.

Turn out the dough onto a well-floured work surface, leave to rest for 2 or 3 minutes, then knead until the dough is smooth and shiny.

Put the dough in a clean bowl, cover the bowl and let the dough rise in a warm place until it doubles in size.

When the dough has doubled in size, knock back and leave to rest for a few minutes, Then turn it out onto a well-floured work surface. Divide the dough into about 18 individual pieces, approximately 50 g/2 oz each. Roll gently into buns.

Place on a lightly floured baking sheet. Cover loosely and allow to rise for about 45 minutes or until the buns have doubled in size.

Dust the buns with flour and bake for 5 minutes then reduce the heat to 200°C/400°F/regulo 6. Cook for a further 10 minutes or until golden. Cool on a wire rack.

Slash the top of each bun with a very sharp knife. Whip the cream until it is fairly stiff and put a dessert spoon of this into each bun. Then top with a teaspoon of raspberry jam. Dust with icing sugar. Yum!

Hot Cross Buns

Hot crossed buns are traditionally eaten in Ireland on Ash Wednesday and Good Friday. The pastry cross on the top each bun represents the crucifixion of Christ.

Makes:	18
Cooking time:	15 minutes, approximately
What you need:	• 450 g/1 lb baker's flour
	• pinch of salt
	• $\frac{1}{4}$ teaspoon cinnamon
	• $\frac{1}{4}$ teaspoon nutmeg
	• 1–2 teaspoons mixed spice
	• 85 g/3 oz castor sugar
	• 85 g/3 oz butter
	• 25 g/1 oz fresh yeast
	• 1 tablespoon castor sugar
	• 50 ml/2 fl oz warm milk
	• 85 g/3 oz currants
	• 225–300 ml/8–10 fl oz tepid milk
	• 50 g/2 oz sultanas
	• 25 g/1 oz chopped peel
	• 2 eggs

Garnish:
- egg wash to glaze, made with milk, sugar and 1 egg yolk
- shortcrust pastry

What you do: Preheat the oven to 220°C/425°F/regulo 7.

In a measuring jug, dissolve the yeast with the tablespoon of castor sugar in 50 ml/2 fl oz of the warm milk.

In a large, wide mixing bowl, sieve in the flour, then add the salt, cinnamon, nutmeg, mixed spice and the 85 g/3 oz sugar. Rub in the butter. Stir in the dried fruits and mix well.

In a bowl, whisk the eggs and the remaining warm milk. Pour this into the measuring jug with the yeast mixture.

Make a well in the centre of the dry ingredients and add the egg, milk and yeast mixture. Combine to a soft dough.

Leave for about 10 minutes. Turn the dough out onto a lightly floured work surface and knead until smooth, then add the currants, sultanas

Cian's Garlic Pizza

Pizza with Red Onions

Timmy's Deep Pan Pizza

Baked Dough Balls

Barrack Bun

Ciabatta

Shaping Ciabatta

and mixed peel. Continue to knead until the dough is smooth and shiny.

Cover the bowl and let the dough rise in a warm place until it doubles in size.

Turn out onto a lightly floured work surface, knock the dough back and leave to rest for a few minutes.

Divide into approximately 18 pieces. Shape into buns. Place them on a baking sheet, egg wash and mark each one carefully by putting a cross of shortcrust pastry on each bun. Allow to rise for about 1 hour and egg wash again.

Bake in a preheated oven for 5 minutes, then reduce the heat to 200°C/400°F/regulo 6 and bake for a further 10 minutes or until golden. Cool on a wire rack.

Serve with soft butter.

Pecan Sticky Buns

These buns are really decadent. And as soon as you take them out of the oven, you will be surrounded and the buns will disappear before they have time to go cold.

Makes:	9
Cooking time:	30–40 minutes
What you need:	• 25 g/1 oz fresh yeast
	• 150 ml/5 fl oz warm water
	• 795 g/1$\frac{3}{4}$ lb strong flour
	• 15 g/$\frac{1}{2}$ oz salt
	• 350 ml/12 fl oz warm water
	• 125 g/4$\frac{1}{2}$ oz unsalted butter
	• 140 g/5 oz dark brown sugar
	• 50 g/2 oz unsalted butter, softened
	• 150 g/5 oz pecan nuts, chopped roughly
	• 70 g/2$\frac{1}{2}$ oz granulated sugar
	• 1 teaspoon ground cinnamon
	• 1 square cake tin, 23 cm/9 in

What you do: Fully preheat the oven to 190°C/375°F/regulo 5.

In a small bowl, sponge the yeast in warm water, leave for about 5 minutes.

In a large, wide bowl, mix the flour and salt together. Make a well in the centre.

Pour the sponged yeast into the flour, mix well together and form a shaggy dough.

Turn out onto a lightly floured work surface and knead for about 5 minutes. The dough should be quite soft.

Cover with a large mixing bowl and leave on the work surface for about 20 minutes to rest.

When the dough is rested, gently knead it on the work surface for another 5 minutes until smooth and shiny.

Put the dough into a lightly oiled, large mixing bowl and turn the dough over in the bowl to coat it with the oil. Cover with clingfilm and leave to rise for about $1\frac{1}{2}$–2 hours, or until it has doubled in size.

While the dough is rising, make the caramel mixture by melting 125 g/$4\frac{1}{2}$ oz of the butter over a low heat and stirring in the brown sugar. Keeping the heat very low, whisk the mixture until silky and turning slightly paler. Take off the heat.

Grease your square cake tin with butter and pour in the caramel mixture. Tilt the tin so as to spread it out evenly.

Sprinkle chopped pecan nuts over the caramel and press them down slightly. Put the tin in the fridge to chill.

Mix the granulated sugar and cinnamon in a bowl. Set aside.

When the dough is doubled in size, knock it back. Flatten into a 33 x 25.5 cm/13 x 10 in rectangle.

Spread the 50 g/2 oz of soft butter evenly over the dough leaving the top 1 cm/$\frac{1}{2}$ in of the dough unbuttered.

Sprinkle the cinnamon sugar evenly over the butter, again leaving the top 1 cm/$\frac{1}{2}$ in bare.

Starting at the bottom, roll up the dough like you would a Swiss roll.

With a metal dough cutter, divide evenly into 9 equal pieces. Lay each piece down in your tin.

Cover and place in a warm position, leave to rise for 1–1½ hours or until the dough is peeping over the top of the tin.

Bake in the preheated oven for 30–40 minutes, or until the buns are golden brown and crusty.

Allow to stand in the tin for 5 minutes, then turn out onto a large serving plate. The gooey, oozy, sticky pecan caramel will spread down over the sides. With a plastic spatula scrape out any of the precious remaining caramel from the tin.

Chocolate Buns

An ideal bun for morning coffee or for children on the run. These buns are made with unsweetened chocolate so I always serve them spread with lashings of delicious home-made chocolate butter (see page 142).

Makes:	24
Cooking time:	15–20 minutes
What you need:	• 350 ml/12 fl oz warm milk
	• 25 g/1 oz fresh yeast
	• 2 teaspoons vanilla essence
	• pinch of salt
	• 85 g/3 oz castor sugar
	• 1 level teaspoon bread soda, finely sieved
	• 570–680 g/1¼–1½ lb strong flour
	• 50 g/2 oz unsweetened chocolate
	• 110 g/4 oz walnuts, finely chopped
	• 2 baking sheets, lightly floured

What you do: Pre-heat oven 190°/375°/regulo 5. Into the bowl of an electric food mixer, crumble the yeast into the warm milk, leave to sponge for about five minutes.

Bring a saucepan half-filled with water to the boil, put a Pyrex or heat-resistant glass bowl over the pan of water, making sure the base of the bowl does not touch the water. Turn off the heat under the saucepan. Leave the chocolate to melt in the bowl.

Add the vanilla, salt, sugar, bread soda and about 310 g/11 oz of flour to the yeast and milk mixture. Beat well with the dough hook.

Add the melted chocolate and beat for a further 2 minutes. Stir in enough of the remaining flour to make a workable dough.

Turn the dough out onto a lightly floured work surface, cover and leave to rest for about 10 minutes.

Knead the dough until it is smooth and elastic, adding more flour if it is too sticky. This will take about 10 minutes.

Leave the dough to rest again for another 5 minutes.

Knead in the walnuts, a few will try to escape as you knead but just push them back in again or eat them!

Place the dough in a large lightly oiled bowl, cover with cling film and leave to rise in a warm place until it has doubled in size.

Knock back and knead for a couple of minutes. Shape into 24 individual buns. Place on the baking sheets, cover and leave to double in size.

Bake for 15–20 minutes. When cooked, the buns will sound hollow when tapped.

Leave to cool on a wire rack. Serve with delicious chocolate butter.

Biscotti

Everyone has their own favourite Biscotti recipe. This one is mine. Biscotti are ideal to keep in a tin in the cupboard as they stay fresh for ages. Certainly longer than they will stay in your tin!

Biscotti are the ideal accompaniment to coffee.

Makes: 48

Cooking time: 25–30 minutes

What you need:
- 70 g/$2\frac{1}{2}$ oz hazelnuts
- 285 g/10 oz plain flour
- 1 teaspoon baking powder
- $\frac{1}{4}$ teaspoon bread soda, finely sieved
- 225 g/8 oz castor sugar
- pinch of salt
- 50 g/2 oz almonds
- 40 g/$1\frac{1}{2}$ oz butter, softened
- 2 eggs
- 1 egg yolk
- 1 teaspoon vanilla essence
- 1 orange, grated zest

What you do: Fully preheat your oven to 180°C/350°F/regulo 4.

On a baking sheet spread the hazelnuts in a single layer and put them into your preheated oven to toast and bring out the flavour of the nuts. This takes about 10 minutes but watch carefully as they can easily burn. The skins will start to crinkle up and blister when they are done.

Remove from the oven and put all the hazelnuts into the centre of a clean tea-towel. Gather up the tea-towel and rub the nuts around in it. This will remove most of the skins. You will not be able to get all of the skins loose, but don't worry.

In a large, wide mixing bowl, sieve the flour, bread soda and baking powder, rub in the butter. Stir in the salt, sugar, hazelnuts and almonds.

In a separate bowl combine eggs, egg yolk, vanilla essence and orange zest. Whisk lightly to combine.

Add the egg mixture to the dry ingredients. Mix together either by hand or with a spatula. It forms quite a stiff dough.

Turn the dough out onto a lightly floured work surface and knead for about 1 minute. Divide the dough into 2 equal portions, roll each one into a log about 30.5 x 2.5 cm/12 x 1 in.

Place the logs on a buttered and floured baking sheet. Leave at least 5 cm/2 in between each log as they will spread as they bake. Press the dough down slightly with the palm of your hand.

Bake for 15–20 minutes, till they are golden brown. Remove from the oven and leave to cool on the baking sheet for about 10 minutes.

Gently lift the logs off the baking sheet onto a chopping board and with a sharp knife cut them at an angle into strips 1 cm/$\frac{1}{2}$ in wide.

Lay each biscotti down flat on the baking sheet and return to your hot oven for a further 10 minutes or until lightly toasted.

Leave to cool completely on the baking sheet. Biscotti can be stored in an airtight tin for up to 1 month.

Serve with strong coffee or with home-made ice cream (page 147).

Doughnuts

What is better than biting through the crunchy sugar coating, into the crisp outer shell and then sinking your teeth into the soft, sweet dough inside. There is no polite way to eat a doughnut. No matter how hard you try, some of the sugar will always find its way onto your cheeks! Still, for me, that's part of the pleasure of eating these decadent delights.

Makes:	18
Cooking time:	4 minutes, approximately
What you need:	• 450 g/1 lb baker's flour
	• pinch of salt
	• 85 g/3 oz castor sugar
	• 85 g/3 oz butter
	• 25 g/1 oz fresh yeast
	• 1 tablespoon of castor sugar
	• 50 ml/2 fl oz warm water
	• 225–300 ml/8–10 fl oz warm water
	• 1 egg

Coating:
- 6 tablespoons castor sugar, mixed with
- 2 tablespoons cinnamon, freshly ground if possible

What you do: Preheat a deep-fat fryer to 190°C/375°F.

In a large, wide mixing bowl, sieve in the flour, add the salt and the 85 g/3 oz castor sugar. Rub in the butter. Mix well.

In a measuring jug, dissolve the yeast with the tablespoon of sugar in the 50 ml/2 fl oz of tepid water.

In a bowl, whisk the egg and add the water, the water should be warm — 'blood heat'. Pour this into the measuring jug with the yeast mixture.

Make a well in the centre of the dry ingredients, pour in the liquid. Mix to a soft dough, adding more liquid if necessary.

Turn the dough out onto a well-floured work surface, leave to rest for 5–10 minutes then knead until the dough is smooth and shiny.

Put the dough in a clean bowl, cover the bowl and let the dough rise in a warm place until it doubles in size.

Then knock back and leave to rest for a few minutes longer. Turn out onto a well-floured work surface.

Divide the dough into 18 individual 25 g/1 oz pieces. Roll each one into a ball, slightly flatten with the palm of your hand. With a floured finger push into the centre. Wriggle your finger around to widen the hole to about to 2 cm/$\frac{3}{4}$ in wide.

Cover loosely with oiled clingfilm and allow to rise for about 45 minutes or until the doughnuts have doubled in size.

Cook in the deep-fat fryer for 1–2 minutes on each side until evenly brown. Drain on kitchen paper.

Roll the doughnuts in castor sugar and ground cinnamon. Serve warm or cold.

Chocolate and Orange Muffins

These tasty muffins are another staple recipe. The beauty of them lies in the fact that once you've made up the batter it can be kept in the fridge for 30 days, so you can bake a few muffins freshly each day!

Makes:	24
Cooking time:	15–20 minutes

What you need:
- 2 eggs
- 310 g/11 oz soft brown sugar
- 400 ml/14 fl oz milk
- 1 teaspoon vanilla essence
- 350 ml/12 fl oz sunflower oil
- 155 g/5$\frac{1}{2}$ oz sultanas
- 85 g/3 oz bran
- 370 g/13 oz plain flour
- $\frac{1}{2}$ teaspoon salt
- 2$\frac{1}{2}$ teaspoons bread soda, finely sieved
- 170 g/6 oz chocolate chips
- 5 oranges, grated zest

What you do: Fully preheat the oven to 200°C/400°F/regulo 6.

In the bowl of an electric mixer, beat the eggs and brown sugar. Add in the milk, vanilla essence, sunflower oil, sultanas, bran, flour, salt and bread soda. Mix until completely blended.

The mixture will be a very wet, gloopy batter, but don't worry.

Take the bowl off the mixer and gently stir in the chocolate chips and the grated orange zest.

Line the muffin trays with muffin cases and fill with the mixture leaving about 1 cm/$\frac{1}{2}$ in below the rim. Bake in the fully preheated oven for approximately 15–20 minutes. Cook until risen and spongy to the touch.

Introduction to
Ethnic Breads

Bread is a truly universal food, found in all cultures. No matter where on the globe you travel, there is almost always some form of native bread. In Ireland we have soda bread made from our soft flour and buttermilk, in Mexico you find tortilla, in India the naan, in Scandinavia the dark rye breads. Most nations also have a flat or unleavened bread: in Ireland the soda bread was sometimes cooked on a griddle over an open fire.

I've been fortunate to have travelled widely over the years and have eaten the breads of many countries. In the school, we also have students of many different nationalities who bring with them treasured recipes from home. Upon returning from a trip abroad I usually head for the kitchen to try and recreate a bread I have eaten while away.

My photo albums are full of holiday snaps but unlike those of most people, scattered amongst pictures of family and friends are photos of the breads we have eaten! Where I was lucky, I have photographs of the breads being prepared, the people who cook them and the ovens the breads were baked in. Travelling through Mexico you find women and children in many street markets making and cooking tortilla and selling them straight from the stove.

On other holidays, I have been lucky enough to meet people who share stories of their own tradition of bread-making. I never cease to be amazed at the diversity of breads found in all cultures and am often reminded too that no matter how far away or how different a culture may be, the basic ingredients for the staple of most national diets remain the same: flour, salt and water.

You will find that some of these recipes mention 'bigas' and 'sponges' to start the dough. You can read all about what they are and what they do in the chapter on Sour Dough (page 121).

Black Bread

I have loved Scandinavian breads ever since I spent a year working on a Danish farm. Here is my version of the traditional Black Bread. We eat it with smoked salmon, gravlax or cold venison.

Makes:	1 loaf
Cooking time:	35–40 minutes

What you need:

Biga:
- 7 g/$\frac{1}{4}$ oz yeast
- 170 ml/6 fl oz water
- 100 g/3$\frac{1}{2}$ oz molasses
- 70 g/2$\frac{1}{2}$ oz strong white flour
- 85 g/3 oz kibbled wheat
- 25 g/1 oz rye flour

Dough:
- 7 g/$\frac{1}{4}$ oz yeast
- 250 g/9 oz rye flour
- 70 g/2$\frac{1}{2}$ oz strong white flour
- 140 g/5 oz wholemeal flour
- 2 teaspoons salt
- 1 tablespoon light muscovado sugar
- 1 tablespoon cocoa
- 170 ml/6 fl oz warm water
- 15 g/$\frac{1}{2}$ oz butter

What you do:

Preheat oven to 180°C/350°F/regulo 4.

First make the biga by soaking together the yeast, warm water and molasses in a glass bowl. Add in the rye flour, white flour and kibbled wheat. Stir together, cover with clingfilm and allow to stand for 12–24 hours until it is really bubbly and active.

Now make the dough. In the bowl of an electric mixer combine the biga with the warm water, sugar and yeast, mix well. Allow to stand for 10 minutes. Add in the flour, salt, cocoa and butter.

Mix this slightly sticky dough until it becomes smooth and elastic, after about 10–15 minutes.

Transfer to an oiled bowl, cover with clingfilm and leave to rise for 2–3 hours or until doubled in size.

Knock the dough back and turn it out onto a lightly floured work surface. Knead for a couple of minutes and then shape the dough to fit your loaf tin.

Cover with a tea-towel and leave to rise for between $1\frac{1}{2}$ and 2 hours or until doubled in size.

Bake in the preheated oven for 35–40 minutes until the loaf is dark brown and sounds hollow when tapped.

Leave to cool on a wire rack. When it completely is completely cold, wrap in clingfilm and leave for at least a day before slicing thinly.

Bread of the Dead

Mexico has been a favourite holiday destination for us as a family. We tend to go in the autumn or at Christmas. We just can't seem to get enough of the colours and flavours of this wonderful country. This particular bread is made for 2nd November to commemorate All Souls' Day. The combination of the richness of the dough with the orange and the aniseed makes an unusual bread. Don't be tempted to substitute the aniseed as the bread won't have the same impact. It will keep for about a week if kept wrapped in clingfilm.

Makes:	4 small loaves
Cooking time:	35–40 minutes
What you need:	**Sponge:**

Sponge:
- 125 ml/4 fl oz water
- 25 g/1 oz yeast
- 1 tablespoon sugar
- 140 g/5 oz strong flour

Dough:
- 2 tablespoons aniseed
- 5 large eggs
- 2 tablespoons orange liqueur
- 110 g/4 oz butter
- 1 orange, grated zest
- 110 g/4 oz sugar
- 2 teaspoons salt
- 450–500 g/1 lb–1 lb 2 oz strong flour

Glaze:
- 110 g/4 oz icing sugar
- 2 3 tablespoons orange liqueur

93

What you do: Preheat oven to 190°C/375°F/regulo 5.

In the bowl of an electric mixer, whisk the water, yeast, sugar and flour. Cover with clingfilm and leave to stand for 1 hour.

In a small saucepan combine the aniseed and water and reduce to about 3 tablespoons of liquid. Strain and leave to cool.

Stir the sponge and add in the eggs, orange liqueur, aniseed water, butter, orange zest, sugar, salt and a third of the flour. Beat on medium speed for about 1 minute or until creamy. Reduce the beater to a low speed and add in the remaining flour.

Turn out the dough onto a lightly floured work surface and knead until soft and smooth, about 1–2 minutes.

Place the dough in a lightly oiled bowl. Cover the bowl with clingfilm and leave to prove for about $1\frac{1}{2}$–2 hours or until doubled in size.

Line a baking sheet with parchment. Turn out onto a lightly floured work surface and divide into 4 equal pieces.

Form into four round loaves, cover loosely and leave to rise for a further 30 minutes. They will not quite double in bulk.

Bake in the centre of your preheated oven for 35–40 minutes. Remove from the tray and leave to cool on a wire rack.

In a small bowl, make the glaze by whisking the icing sugar and orange liqueur. Beat to form a glaze that is smooth and thick but pourable.

Pour the glaze over the surface of the still hot loaf, let the extra drip down over the sides. Leave to cool on a wire rack before slicing.

Chinese Wok Bread

Sitting on the steps of a café late one evening while visiting the Manya Ruins of Tekal in Guatemala, Christmas 1996, I got chatting to a Chinese American who had fond memories as a little girl of helping her grandmother make bread in a bamboo steamer over a wok. Her family have long since lost the recipe. As we chatted she recalled very clearly how her grandmother mixed the dough, kneaded it, proved it, knocked it back, then shaped the little buns of dough. She could remember how each bun was placed gently into the steamer, let rise again and then finally the steamer was placed over simmering water in the wok. What she loved most was when the bread was cooked that way she could peel it layer by layer, prolonging the pleasure.

I began to visualise how I might make this bread. When I got home I tried my ideas. This is my version of Chinese bread for you.

Makes: 7 soft buns

Cooking time: 1 hour, approximately

What you need:
- 15 g/$\frac{1}{2}$ oz fresh yeast
- 200 ml/7 fl oz water
- 25 g/1 oz butter
- 1 teaspoon salt
- 15 g/$\frac{1}{2}$ oz sugar
- 450 g/1 lb strong white flour

- bamboo steamer, 30 cm/12 in
- wok

What you do: Sponge the yeast in 150 ml/5 fl oz lukewarm water. Set aside for about 10 minutes. Add the remaining lukewarm water.

In a large, wide bowl, mix the flour with the salt and sugar. Make a well in the centre and pour in most of the lukewarm liquid.

Mix to a loose dough, adding the remainder of the liquid, or more flour or liquid as necessary.

Turn the dough out onto a lightly floured work surface, cover and leave to relax for about 5 minutes.

Then knead for about 10 minutes or until smooth, springy and elastic. If kneading in a food mixer with a dough hook, 5 minutes is usually long enough.

Put the dough in a ceramic bowl. Cover the top tightly with clingfilm.

Rising time depends on the temperature, but the bread will taste better if it rises more slowly.

When the dough has more than doubled in size, knock it back. Leave it to relax again for 10 minutes.

Shape the bread into 7 balls of dough and transfer these to the middle section of the bamboo steamer, placing each ball of dough on a disc of baking parchment about 5 cm/2 in wide, and cover with a tea-towel.

Allow to rise again in a warm place. This rising will be shorter, only about 20–30 minutes. The bread is ready to be steamed when a small dent remains when you press the dough lightly with your finger. Sprinkle with a little more flour.

Have a wok ready on a high heat, filled with water so that the level reaches up over the base of the bamboo steamer. The water should be simmering. Put the middle of the bamboo steamer gently into the wok. Keep an eye on the water level in the wok so that it does not boil dry.

The bread takes exactly 1 hour to cook. *Do not under any circumstances* lift the lid off the steamer while it is cooking or the bread will collapse.

Ciabatta

Here is my own adaptation of the recipe from Carol Field's wonderful book, *The Italian Baker*. This is a bread well worth the effort and bears little resemblance to its commercial counterparts. It is a surprising bread with a soft, crisp crust concealing an open, chewy-textured loaf within. Split it in half and eat with cheese or any filling of your choice.

Makes:	4–10 loaves
Cooking time:	20–25 minutes
What you need:	**Biga:**

- 7 g/$\frac{1}{4}$ oz yeast
- 400 ml/14 fl oz warm water
- 500 g/1 lb 2 oz plain flour

Ciabatta:
- 7 g/$\frac{1}{4}$ oz fresh yeast
- 125 ml/4 fl oz warm milk
- 300 ml/10 fl oz warm water
- 1 tablespoon olive oil
- 475–600 ml/17–20 fl oz biga
- 500 g/1 lb 2 oz plain flour
- 15 g/$\frac{1}{2}$ oz salt

What you do: Preheat the oven to 220C/425F/regulo 7.

Make the biga by stirring the yeast into 50 ml/2 fl oz warm water and leave until creamy, about 10 minutes. Stir in the remaining water and then the flour.

Put the biga into a lightly oiled bowl, cover with clingfilm and let rise at room temperature for 12–24 hours.

It will more than double in volume and will be wet and sticky. It will also have a very strong fermented smell when ready.

The next day, stir the yeast into the warm milk in the bowl of an electric mixer, let it stand for about 10 minutes. Add the water, oil and biga.

Mix with the paddle until blended. Add the flour and salt, mix for 10 minutes. Change to the dough hook and beat for 15–25 minutes at high speed, or until the dough is stringy and pulling away from the sides of the bowl. Getting the dough to this stage is essential for final shaping of the bread.

Place the dough in an oiled bowl, cover with clingfilm, leave to rise for 1–1$\frac{1}{2}$ hours or until the dough has doubled in size. The dough should be full of air bubbles, very supple, elastic and sticky when fully risen. **Don't** knock the dough back.

Turn the dough out onto a well-floured work surface. Cut the dough into 4–10 pieces depending on what size you prefer and what occasion you are making the bread for. Generously flour 2 baking trays. Place the pieces onto the tray.

Dimple the loaves with the tips of your fingers.

Cover with tea-towels and leave to rest until puffy, for 30–45 minutes. The loaves will not have risen much but when pressed with a finger will still be quite active. Dust lightly with flour before baking for 20–25 minutes. Cool on wire racks.

Freemantle Flat Bread

Christmas, 1999. Darina and I decided we would pay a surprise visit to our daughters who were travelling in Australia. We had not seen Lydia for nearly a year. She had been in Australia since the previous Easter. She was ecstatic when she saw us. Emily, on the other hand, was rather dubious when she joined her sister a few days later only to find Mum and Dad in tow! Lydia was working at the time in the Kidogo Art Centre in Freemantle, outside Perth. This is where I discovered this unusual flat bread, served in the many cafés and restaurants that dot the city. It is great eaten cut into wedges with salads and grilled meats or fish.

Makes:	5 pieces
Cooking time:	next to no time

What you need:
- 500 g/1 lb 2 oz strong white flour
- 250 ml/9 fl oz water
- pinch of sugar
- 1 teaspoon salt
- rice flour for rolling
- olive oil
- Maldon sea salt and freshly ground pepper

What you do: Into the bowl of an electric mixer, put in the flour, water and butter. Add in the sugar and salt. Mix together at a slow speed with a dough hook.

Continue to mix until the dough is really smooth and shiny, about 5 minutes.

Turn onto a lightly floured work surface and knead gently for a couple of minutes. Roll the dough into a cylinder and wrap in greaseproof paper. Refrigerate over night.

The following day, after the dough has rested, divide into 5 equal pieces.

Dust a work surface with rice flour. Roll each portion out into a very thin disc. Don't worry too much about the shape of the disc, as long as it is thin.

Cover and leave to rest for about 20 minutes.

Brush the breads with olive oil and sprinkle with salt and freshly ground black pepper.

Preheat your grill to its highest setting then grill one or two flat breads at a time. They will puff up almost immediately. Be careful not to overcook or they will become brittle and crisp.

Wrap in a warm tea-towel until serving.

Lovisa's Swedish Crisp Bread

On our 12-week course at the Ballymaloe Cookery School, we have students of many different nationalities. We always encourage them to make their own ethnic bread. Some students, like Lovisa, a young Swedish girl, are often homesick for the breads of their own country and are thrilled to get the chance. I made these super-light and crunchy crisp breads with Lovisa, and she was surprised when I had a traditional Scandinavian knackeboard rolling pin. The wood on the pin is criss-cross scored on the surface. When you roll out the dough, it pricks the surface and gives a textured finish.

These crisp breads are ideal for eating with cheese and keep for weeks if stored in an airtight container.

Makes:	10
Cooking time:	10–15 minutes
What you need:	• 1 teaspoon caraway seeds
	• 25 g/1 oz fresh yeast
	• 300 ml/10 fl oz milk
	• 310 g/11 oz plain rye flour
	• 310 g/11 oz strong white flour
	• 1 teaspoon salt
	• 2.5 cm/1 in cutter
What you do:	Preheat the oven to 180°C/350°F/regulo 4.

Grind the caraway seeds finely. Crumble the yeast into a bowl and pour the warm milk over it and leave to sponge for 5 minutes.

Mix the flour with the salt and caraway seeds. Sprinkle onto the liquid. Bring together to form a soft dough.

Turn onto a lightly floured work surface and knead for 5 minutes. Roll into a cylinder and divide into 10 equal pieces.

Shape each piece into a ball, cover and leave to rise for 20 minutes.

Sprinkle a work surface lightly with rye flour. Roll out each ball with a smooth rolling pin to 20 cm/8 in, turning the dough as you roll to keep it round.

Prick all over with a fork or if you have a traditional knackeboard rolling pin use this instead.

Stamp out a little hole in the centre of each crisp bread with 2.5 cm/ 1 in cutter.

Preheat a lightly oiled baking sheet. Place the crisp bread on the hot baking sheet and bake for 10–15 minutes.

No need to waste the little centre pieces of dough. Cook them as well as they are super as tiny cheese biscuits.

Eat warm or cold.

Naan Bread

Naan bread, probably the most often eaten and widely known of all Indian breads. It is a wonderful soft-textured bread ideal for eating with any spicy dish. When my daughter-in-law Penny makes these naan breads, she often kneads a different flavour into each one. Poppy seeds into the first, cumin in the second, garlic in the third, and so on. Penny has even on occasion put in grated chocolate!

Makes:	6–8
Cooking time:	3–4 minutes each, or two at a time
What you need:	• 150 ml/5 fl oz tepid milk • 2 teaspoons castor sugar • 2 teaspoons dried active yeast • 450 g/1 lb plain flour • $\frac{1}{2}$ teaspoon salt • 1 teaspoon baking powder • 2 tablespoons vegetable oil, plus a little extra • 150 ml/5 fl oz plain yoghurt, lightly beaten • 1 egg, lightly beaten
What you do:	Preheat your oven to 230°C/450°F/regulo 8. Put the warmed milk in a bowl. Add 1 teaspoon of the sugar and the yeast. Mix well and leave to sponge for 15–20 minutes. Into a large, wide bowl, sift the flour, salt and baking powder. Add the remaining 1 teaspoon sugar, the yeast mixture, the 2 tablespoons of vegetable oil, the yoghurt and the egg.

Mix and form a ball of dough.

Turn the dough out onto a lightly floured work surface and knead it for about 10 minutes or until it is smooth and satiny.

Oil a large bowl. Put the dough into the bowl and turn the dough so it is coated lightly all over with oil. Cover the bowl with a piece of clingfilm and set aside in a warm, draught-free place for 1 hour or until the dough has doubled in bulk.

Put your heaviest baking tray in the oven to heat. Preheat your grill.

Knock back the dough and knead it again. Divide it into 6 equal balls. Keep 5 of them covered while you work with the other. The dough will be really soft.

Roll each ball into a teardrop-shaped naan, about 25.5 cm/10 in long and about 13 cm/5 in at its widest end.

If you want to add any spices or seeds put them into the centre of the naan at this stage, parcel the dough around it. Roll up the dough and shape.

Remove the hot baking tray from the oven and put the naan onto the tray. It is possible to cook two naan breads on the one baking tray. Put it immediately into the oven for 3 minutes. It will puff up.

Now place the baking tray under the grill, about 7.5–10 cm/3–4 in away from the heat, for about 30 seconds or until the top of the naans browns slightly.

Wrap the naans in a clean tea-towel to keep the crust soft and warm. Make all the naans this way and serve warm.

Penny's Perthshire Butteries

My son Toby recently married a bonnie Scottish lass who recalls fighting over the butteries on Sunday mornings at breakfast in boarding school. There were never enough of these rich buttery treats to go around. So, in Penny's honour, I have named my own version just for her.

Makes:	20 butteries
Cooking time:	20–25 minutes
What you need:	• 680 g/1$\frac{1}{2}$ lb strong white flour • 15 g/$\frac{1}{2}$ oz salt • 425 ml/15 fl oz water • 25 g/1 oz yeast • 1 tablespoon sugar • 340 g/12 oz butter, softened • 3 lightly floured baking sheets
What you do:	Preheat the oven to 200°C/400°F/regulo 6.

Sieve the flour and salt together into a large, wide mixing bowl. Make a well in the centre.

Into a measuring jug, crumble the yeast and cream in the sugar. Add the warm water and mix to a smooth liquid.

Pour this yeast liquid into the flour and work it to a soft but not sticky dough.

Turn this dough onto a lightly floured work surface and knead for about 10 minutes. When the dough has been kneaded enough it will be smooth, shiny and springy to the touch.

Put the dough in a large clean and, if possible, ceramic mixing bowl. Cover with a tea-towel and leave in a warm place to rise for about 1$\frac{1}{2}$–2 hours or until the mixture has doubled in size.

When the dough is risen, knock it back. Roll out the dough on a lightly floured work surface into a rectangle approximately 45 x 15 cm/6 x 18 in. Divide the softened butter into 3 equal portions. Spread the top two-thirds of the dough rectangle with one portion of the butter. Fold the unbuttered part of the dough over half of the buttered dough, then fold the other half of the buttered dough over to make a 3-layered sandwich.

Seal the edges by pressing down on them with a rolling pin. Wrap the dough in clingfilm and chill in the fridge for 30 minutes.

Remove from the fridge and repeat the rolling, folding and chilling twice more. Always roll the dough out with the enclosed side to your left. This helps to capture and keep the precious air that gives the butteries their lightness.

Take the dough out of the fridge again, turn onto a floured work surface and roll out to about 1 cm–$\frac{1}{2}$ in high. Leave to rest uncovered for 5 minutes. Using a metal dough cutter lightly dusted with flour, cut the butteries into 20 squares or more.

Place the cut butteries upside down and spaced well apart on the baking sheets. Cover with a tea-towel and prove for a further 20 minutes.

Bake the butteries in your fully preheated oven for 20–25 minutes until golden brown and crispy on top.

Cool on a wire rack.

Serve warm for breakfast with home-made raspberry jam (page 140) and butter.

Pitta Bread

Easier to make than you might imagine, pitta bread is so versatile, you can stuff it with salad, spiced beef, cheese or just eat them on their own. Once you have made your own pitta bread it will be hard to go back to anything else.

Makes:	8
Cooking time:	8 minutes, approximately
What you need:	• 400 g/14 oz strong white flour
	• 2 teaspoons salt
	• 1 tablespoon sugar
	• 15 g/$\frac{1}{2}$ oz yeast
	• 2 tablespoons olive oil
	• 225 ml/8 fl oz hot water
	• 8 squares of aluminium foil, 18 cm/7 in each
What you do:	Preheat the oven to 250°C/475°F/regulo 9.

Into the bowl of an electric mixer, put 110 g/4 oz of the flour. Mix in the salt and sugar, crumble in the yeast. Add the oil and hot water. Blend at a low speed with the paddle of the mixer for 30 seconds.

Now change to the dough hook, mix in the balance of the flour, spooning in 2 tablespoons at a time. Keeping the mixer motor running. When all the flour has been added knead for a further 4–5 minutes. The dough will be a shaggy mass. Continue to knead until the dough comes easily away from the sides of the bowl.

Turn the dough out onto a lightly floured work surface. Knead by hand for a couple of minutes. The dough will be slightly sticky.

Divide the dough into 8 pieces. Roll into balls, cover and leave to rest for 20 minutes.

With the palm of your hand gently flatten each ball. Roll out to a disc about 15 cm/6 in wide and 5 mm/$\frac{1}{4}$ in thick.

With pitta bread it is much more important to get the discs thin, so don't worry too much about getting a perfect circle.

Put each disc of dough onto the aluminium foil. Leave to rest for a further 5 minutes while you preheat a baking sheet.

To bake, carefully put 2 or 3 of the breads onto the hot baking sheet and bake in the oven for approximately 8 minutes or until they have puffed up. Repeat with the remaining discs. The pitta bread should only be a very light golden colour. If you allow them get too dark they will have a hard crust and be too dry.

When you take the bread from the oven, wrap them in aluminium foil. The tops will fall and you will have a pocket that you can fill. Serve warm or cold.

Poori

Another super Indian bread. Lots of fun to make with all the family or with friends because of the dramatic effect when they cook. The pooris resemble blown-up balloons so children love them. They cook magically in hardly any time and are great if you want a change from naan bread. Or if you are feeling adventurous, why not make both?

I really recommend that if you are making these you use a deep-fat fryer as the oil needs to be very hot. With a deep-fat fryer you can control the temperature and so the risk of a kitchen fire is seriously reduced.

Makes:	12
Cooking time:	just a few seconds each
What you need:	• 110 g/4 oz wholemeal flour
	• 110 g/4 oz plain flour
	• $\frac{1}{2}$ teaspoon salt
	• 2 tablespoons vegetable oil
	• 100 ml/$3\frac{1}{2}$ fl oz water
	• deep-fat fryer
What you do:	Preheat the deep-fat fryer to 190°C/375°F.

Into a large bowl, place the two flours and the salt. Dribble the 2 tablespoons of oil over the top. Rub the oil in with your fingers so the mixture resembles coarse breadcrumbs. Slowly add the water to form a ball of dough.

Turn the dough out onto a very lightly floured work surface. Knead it for 10–12 minutes or until it is smooth.

Rub about $\frac{1}{4}$ teaspoon oil on the ball and put the dough into a clean ceramic bowl, not plastic, and cover with clingfilm. Set aside to rest for 30 minutes.

Knead the dough again, and divide it into 12 equal pieces. Keep 11 of them covered while you work with the other.

Flatten each ball in turn and roll it out into a 13–14 cm/5–5$\frac{1}{2}$ in round. When they are all rolled out, keep the pooris in a single layer, covered with clingfilm.

Lift up one poori and lay it carefully over the surface of the hot oil in the deep-fat fryer. It might sink to the bottom but it should rise in seconds and begin to sizzle. Using the back of a slotted metal spoon, push the poori gently into the oil with tiny, swift strokes.

Within seconds, the poori will puff up. Turn it over and cook the other side for about 10 seconds.

Remove it from the hot oil and put it on the plate lined with kitchen paper.

Cook all the pooris in this way.

Serve the pooris hot as a great accompaniment to and Indian curry or any spicy Indian dish.

Tortillas

Mexican food seems to get more and more popular. Making your own tortillas could not be easier. Perfect for using in burritos, fajitas, quesadilla and a host of other Mexican dishes.

Makes:	about 25, 24 cm/9 in wide
Cooking time:	up to 1 minute each
What you need:	• 450 g/1 lb plain flour
	• 1 dessertspoon salt
	• 85 g/3 oz butter
	• 225 ml/8 fl oz warm water
What you do:	Sieve the flour and salt together in a bowl, rub in the butter. Add warm water slowly; the amount you need may vary with the type of flour used.

Turn the dough onto a lightly floured work surface and knead it until it is no longer sticky. Keep the dough covered with a warm, damp cloth.

Take approximately 25 g/1 oz dough at a time and knead each piece, folding it in on itself to trap air in for a few seconds. Now make it into a little ball and flatten it out.

Place the flattened ball on a floured work surface, and roll it out with a rolling pin until it is so thin that you can see the work surface through it. Without greasing it, heat a heavy-bottomed frying pan on a moderate heat until a drop of water will sizzle in it.

Pop a tortilla straight onto the pan, cook for 30 seconds on one side then turn over, and cook for 15–30 seconds on the other. Cover with a tea-towel and keep them warm or store in a tortilla basket if you have one.

To freeze flour tortillas, place waxed or greaseproof paper between them, as they tend to stick together, especially when frozen. They defrost easily if left at room temperature for 30 minutes.

Introduction to
Flavoured and
Speciality
Breads

There are times when you want to impress, whether you are cooking a meal for friends, or perhaps you just want to try something different. I hope this chapter will take what you have learned so far in this book and put an exciting twist on it.

The range of breads introduced here all have their own distinct and definite flavour. Some are sweet, but for the most part they are savoury. Though some have an ethnic origin, I have kept them separate from the 'Ethnic Breads' because they all share one thing in common. That is the fact that they have a dominant flavour — whether the result of their main ingredient or not — and it is this special flavour element that makes you stop and say *Mmmmmm*.

Garlic and Mozzarella Stromboli

This is an Italian bread that is a bread and a sandwich all in one. The dough is baked with a cheese and sausage filling. It is then served in thick slices. Often we take it on a picnic as it is so easy to handle and is a lot less bother than sandwiches. You can vary the filling with any combination of cheeses. Sometimes I add crispy bacon instead of the spicy sausage or even a little fresh chilli if you want some extra kick.

Makes:	1 loaf
Cooking time:	40–45 minutes
What you need:	• 15 g/$\frac{1}{2}$ oz fresh yeast
	• 1 teaspoon honey
	• 70 g/2$\frac{1}{2}$ oz wholemeal flour
	• 225 ml/8 fl oz tepid water
	• 1 egg
	• 2 tablespoons extra virgin olive oil
	• 1 teaspoon salt
	• 340 g/12 oz strong white flour

Filling:
- 170 g/6 oz grated mozzarella
- 50 g/2 oz grated Parmesan
- 50 g/2 oz spicy chorizo sausage, chopped
- 2 tablespoons flat leaf parsley, chopped
- 2 tablespoons chives, chopped
- 2 large cloves of garlic, crushed
- 1 egg
- 1 teaspoon salt
- freshly ground black pepper

What you do: Preheat the oven to 220°C/425°F/regulo 7.

In a small bowl, sponge the yeast in the tepid water with the honey and 1 tablespoon of wholemeal flour. Leave in a warm place for about 5–10 minutes.

Into the bowl of an electric mixer, pour the egg, oil, salt, the rest of the wholemeal flour and 4 tablespoons of the strong flour, pour in the yeast mixture. Whisk on high speed until smooth. Add the remaining strong flour a few spoons at a time.

The dough should be smooth and elastic. Turn it out onto a lightly floured work surface and knead for about 3 minutes. Put the dough into a lightly oiled ceramic bowl, cover with clingfilm. Leave to rise for about 1 hour or until doubled in size.

While the dough is rising, make the filling. Mix all the ingredients together and set aside until needed.

Knock the dough back and turn it out onto a lightly floured work surface. Roll out into a rectangle 30 x 40 cm/12 x 16 in. Spread the filling over the dough leaving about 2.5 cm/1 in around the edge.

Roll up the dough like you would a Swiss roll, starting with one of the long sides. Pinch along the seams to seal in the filling.

Carefully transfer to a lined baking sheet seam side down. Cover with clingfilm and leave to rest for 30 minutes.

Brush the top of the loaf with olive oil and prick all over with a skewer. Bake in the centre of a hot oven for 15 minutes. Reduce the temperature to 190°C/375°F/regulo 5 and bake for a further 25–30 minutes.

Cool on the baking tray for 10 minutes and then transfer to a wire rack.

Mango Bread

Another bread from Mexico. Our youngest daughter Emily has always had a passion for mangoes, so when I made this bread it was her opinion I really valued. Yes, she approved. Like eating a fresh mango, this bread fizzes on your tongue in the most startling way.

Makes: 2 loaves

Cooking time: 35–40 minutes

What you need:
- 285 g/10 oz plain flour
- 2 teaspoons cinnamon
- 2 teaspoons bread soda, finely sieved
- $\frac{1}{2}$ teaspoon salt
- 85 g/3 oz raisins
- 200 g/7 oz castor sugar
- 2 eggs
- 1 teaspoon pure vanilla extract
- 2 large mangoes, pealed and chopped
- 1 tablespoon lime juice

- 2 loaf tins, fully lined

Lime glaze:
- 140 g/5 oz icing sugar
- 25 g/1 oz butter
- 1 lime, grated zest
- 3 tablespoons lime juice

What you do: Preheat the oven to 180°C/350°F/regulo 4.

In a large, wide mixing bowl, combine the flour, cinnamon, bread soda and salt.

In another bowl, whisk the sugar and eggs until pale and fluffy, approximately 3 minutes.

Gently fold the flour into the egg mixture. Be careful not to over-mix it.

Stir in the chopped mangoes, raisins and lime juice.

Divide the batter between the two tins. Bake in the preheated oven for 35–40 minutes or until a skewer inserted into the centre of each loaf comes out clean.

Make the lime glaze by whisking all the ingredients together until smooth. Pour the glaze over the loaves while still warm.

Quick Fig Bread

If you like figs, you will love this bread. A great energy loaf packed with nutritious figs and currants. Ideal for breakfast or your mid-morning snack. Don't be put off by the length of the list of ingredients, it truly is a quick bread!

Makes: 1 loaf

Cooking time: 1 hour 20 minutes, approximately

What you need:
- 140 g/5 oz plain flour
- 140 g/5 oz rye flour
- 70 g/$2\frac{1}{2}$ oz wholemeal flour
- 7 g/$\frac{1}{4}$ oz bran
- 15 g/$\frac{1}{2}$ oz light brown sugar
- 2 teaspoons baking powder
- 1 teaspoon bread soda, finely sieved
- 1$\frac{1}{2}$ teaspoons instant espresso powder
- 1$\frac{1}{2}$ teaspoons unsweetened cocoa powder
- $\frac{1}{2}$ teaspoon salt
- 225 g/8 oz dried figs, roughly chopped
- 25 g/1 oz currants
- 225 ml/8 fl oz buttermilk
- 63 ml/$2\frac{1}{2}$ fl oz sour cream
- 50 g/2 oz butter melted
- 1 egg
- 2 tablespoons treacle

- 1 loaf tin, oiled

What you do: Preheat your oven to 180°C/350°F/regulo 4.

In a large, wide mixing bowl, combine the flours, bran, brown sugar, baking powder, bread soda, espresso powder, cocoa powder and salt. Add the figs and currants and toss all the ingredients together until they are evenly distributed. Make a well in the centre.

Melt the butter.

In a measuring jug, mix the buttermilk, sour cream, egg and treacle. Add in the melted butter and whisk with a fork until frothy.

Pour the buttermilk mixture into the dry ingredients. Stir gently with a wooden spoon until evenly mixed. The batter will be very thick. Pour into the loaf tin.

Bake in your preheated oven for about 1 hour and 20 minutes or until a skewer inserted into the centre comes out clean.

Leave to cool in the tin. Serve with butter for a breakfast full of energy.

Rye and Caraway Loaf

Delicious bread with cold meats, ideal to have at a buffet.

Makes:	2–3 small loaves
Cooking time:	30–45 minutes
What you need:	• 25 g/1 oz fresh yeast
	• 300 ml/10 fl oz warm water
	• 340 g/12 oz strong white flour
	• 140 g/5 oz dark rye flour
	• 25 g/1 oz caraway seeds
	• 1 teaspoon salt
	• 50 g/2 oz butter
What you do:	Preheat oven to 230°C/450°F/regulo 8.

Dissolve the yeast in the warm water. Leave aside for about 10 minutes.

In a large, wide mixing bowl, combine the flours, caraway seeds and salt. Make a well in the centre.

Add the liquid yeast to the dry ingredients. Mix to a good, soft, but not sticky, dough. You may need to add a little extra warm water.

Turn out onto a lightly floured work surface. Add butter and knead until smooth, about 10 minutes.

Place in a large bowl. Cover and leave to rise in a warm place. When it has doubled in size, knock it back and shape into 2 or 3 loaves. Cover and leave to rise again.

When the loaves have doubled in size, brush them with egg wash, sprinkle with caraway seeds and slash the tops across with a sharp knife.

Bake in the preheated oven for about 30–45 minutes depending on size, or until the bread sounds hollow when tapped.

Cool on a wire rack.

Sfinciuni

I run a bread course each spring here in the school. My daughter-in-law Rachel demonstrates with me. We always have lots of craic together teaching this course. When the time comes to do sfinciuni I always turn around to find Rachel as I can never pronounce the name of this bread properly. To tease me Rachel stays silent so I have to ask her in front of the class to pronounce it for me!

Makes: 1 pie

Cooking time: 20 minutes, approximately

What you need:
- 200 g/7 oz white yeast dough (see page 38)
- 110 g/4 oz mozzarella cheese, roughly grated, soaked in 2 tablespoons olive oil for 1 hour
- 15 g/$\frac{1}{2}$ oz Parmesan cheese, freshly grated
- 3 tablespoons Timmy's Tomato Fondue (see page 145)
- 1 dessertspoon parsley, freshly chopped
- 1 dessertspoon basil, freshly chopped
- 2–4 anchovies and/or 6–8 black olives, stoned and halved
- semolina
- olive oil for brushing

What you do: Preheat the oven to 250°C/475°F/regulo 9.

Divide the dough in half. On a lightly floured work surface, roll out to 20 cm, 8 inches piece as thinly as possible.

Sprinkle semolina over the pizza paddle or baking tray and arrange the dough on top. Mix the ingredients together and spread on the dough base to within 2 cm/$\frac{1}{2}$ in of the edge. Dampen the edges with cold water.

Roll out the remainder of the dough and put on top, seal and crimp the edges.

Brush with cold water and slide into the fully preheated oven. Bake for 20 minutes or until crisp and golden. Brush with olive oil and serve immediately with a tasty green salad.

Chinese Wok Bread

Penny's Perthshire Butteries

Tomato and Fennel Bread

Basic Potato Starter

French Toast

Shannon Chicken Casserole

Vanilla Bread with Chocolate Butter

Prepping Isaac's Roasted Tomato Sauce

Three-Cheese Spirals

A tasty, cheesy snack that looks incredible.

Makes:	15
Cooking time:	20–25 minutes
What you need:	• 15 g/$\frac{1}{2}$ oz yeast
	• 450 g/1 lb strong flour
	• 2 teaspoons salt
	• 63 ml/2$\frac{1}{2}$ fl oz warm milk
	• 125 ml/4 fl oz warm water
	• olive oil
	• 1 tablespoon marjoram, chopped
	• 3 eggs
	• 1 baking tray, lined with parchment paper
	Filling:
	• 50 g/2 oz mature cheddar cheese, grated
	• 25 g/1 oz Parmesan cheese, grated
	• 50 g/2 oz goat's cheese
	• 2 tablespoons olive oil

What you do:

Fully preheat the oven to 180°C/350°F/regulo 4.

In the bowl of an electric mixer fitted with the paddle attachment, mix the yeast and 225 g/8 oz of the flour with the salt, warm water and milk. Beat for approximately 1 minute until creamy. Add the marjoram and eggs. Add the remaining flour and continue to beat until the dough is just coming away from the sides of the bowl.

Turn the dough out onto a lightly floured work surface and knead for 2 minutes.

Put the dough into a lightly oiled bowl, cover with clingfilm and leave in a warm place for 1–1$\frac{1}{2}$ hours, or until doubled in size.

While the dough is rising, make the filling by mixing the cheeses together, adding the olive oil and then blending to a smooth paste. Knock the dough back and turn it out onto a lightly floured work surface. Roll out the pieces of dough into a large 30 x 45 cm/ 16 x 18 in rectangle. Spread the cheese filling.

Starting from one of the long edges roll up the dough like a Swiss roll.

Using a serrated edge knife, cut 15 thick slices. Then take 1 slice at a time and with a gentle sawing motion cut into the centre two-thirds of the way down so the roll falls open into a double snail. Do this with all the rolls.

Gently place each double snail on the lined baking tray. Leave at least 5 cm/2 in between each roll, as they expand a lot.

Cover loosely with clingfilm and leave to rise for 1 hour, or until just doubled in size.

Bake in the fully preheated oven for 20–25 minutes. The rolls will be golden brown and puffy.

Serve warm.

Tomato and Fennell Bread

It's hard to resist a tomato bread and this one is no exception. The addition of fennel to my mind adds a truly great dimension.

Makes:	2 loaves
Cooking time:	30–35 minutes
What you need:	• 680 g/ 1½ lb strong white flour
	• 25 g/1 oz yeast
	• 2 level teaspoons salt
	• 150 ml/5 fl oz very hot water
	• 15 g/½ oz sugar
	• 25 g/1 oz butter
	• 250 ml/9 fl oz lukewarm water, more as needed
	• 2 tablespoons tomato paste
	• 1 tablespoon fennel seeds

Topping:
• egg wash
• fennell seeds, optional, for sprinkling

What you do: Fully preheat oven to 230°C/450°F/regulo 8.

In a glass jug, mix the yeast with 125 ml/4 fl oz lukewarm water until dissolved.

Put the butter, salt, sugar and tomato paste into a bowl with the 150 ml/5 fl oz of very hot water, stir until the butter is melted.

Add 150 ml/5 fl oz of the lukewarm water. By now, the liquid should be lukewarm or blood heat, so combine this with the yeast mixture.

Sieve the flour into a large, wide mixing bowl, add the fennel seeds and make a well in the centre. Pour in enough tomato/yeast mixture to mix to a loose dough. Add more flour or warm water as necessary.

Turn out the dough onto a lightly floured work surface, cover and leave to relax for 5–10 minutes.

Then knead for about 10 minutes or until smooth and springy. If kneading in a food mixer with a dough hook, 5 minutes should be long enough.

Put the dough to rise in a ceramic bowl and cover tightly with clingfilm. Leave in a warm place $1\frac{1}{2}$–2 hours, or until the dough has doubled in size.

Knock back the dough. Turn out onto a lightly floured work surface, cover and leave to relax again for 10 minutes.

Shape the bread into loaves, plaits or rolls and cover with a tea-towel.

Allow to rise again in a warm place, this rising will be much shorter, only about 20–30 minutes.

The dough is ready for baking when a small dent remains when pressed lightly with the finger. Brush with egg wash and sprinkle with fennel seeds.

Bake in a hot oven for 30–35 minutes.

Walnut Bread

If you have ever travelled in France you are sure to remember being served walnut bread as an accompaniment to cheese. If you have guests to impress, this bread is ideal to have at a dinner party. It can also be shaped into buns before the second rising to make individual servings.

Makes:	2 loaves
Cooking time:	30 minutes, approximately

What you need:
- 340 g/12 oz strong white flour
- 110 g/4 oz strong brown flour
- 1 teaspoon salt
- 3 tablespoons olive oil
- 25 g/1 oz yeast
- 2 teaspoons sugar
- 200 ml/7 fl oz warm water
- 110 g/4 oz walnuts, roughly chopped
- 25 g/1 oz raisins
- 1 tablespoons olive oil

What you do: Preheat the oven to 230°C/450°F/regulo 8.

In a small bowl, mix the yeast with the sugar and 150 ml/5 fl oz of the water. Leave for 3–4 minutes in a warm place until the yeast starts to work.

Put the flour and salt in a large bowl with the olive oil.

Pour the yeast mixture into the flour, add the remaining water and mix to a pliable dough.

Knead for about 10 minutes or until the dough is smooth and elastic, then knead in the walnuts and raisins.

Put the dough in a lightly oiled bowl. Cover the bowl with a damp cloth or clingfilm and leave the dough to rise in a warm place for about $1\frac{1}{2}$ hours, or until it doubles in bulk.

Knock back the dough. Turn it out onto a lightly floured work surface and knead for 3 or 4 minutes.

Divide into 2 balls or shape them any way you like. Place on an oiled baking tray. Cover and let the dough rise for about 1 hour or until it has doubled in size.

Brush the loaves with water to soften the crust and bake for about 30 minutes, or until they sound hollow when tapped on the bottom. Cooking time will vary depending on the size of the loaves you choose to make.

Once out of the oven, brush with the remaining olive oil and cool on a wire rack.

Zucchini Bread

For many years, friends of ours from the United States, the Comptons, come and spend a few weeks here in the summer. They love the peace and quite of East Cork. Diana Compton has often said that we should make zucchini bread with the wonderful sweet crop of zucchini we have in the glasshouse. Last year Diana gave me her family recipe for the bread, and this is my version of her American classic.

Makes:	2 loaves
Cooking time:	50–60 minutes
What you need:	• 450 g/1 lb plain flour
	• 1 teaspoon baking powder
	• 1 level teaspoon bread soda, finely sieved
	• 1 teaspoon salt
	• 2 teaspoons cinnamon
	• 1 teaspoon nutmeg
	• $\frac{1}{2}$ teaspoon ground cloves
	• 125 ml/4 fl oz milk
	• 2 eggs
	• 110 g/4 oz butter
	• 110 g/4 oz sugar
	• 3 zucchini, 15 cm/6 in, grated
	• 50 g/ 2 oz chopped walnuts
	• 2 loaf tins, fully lined

What you do: Fully preheat the oven to 180°C/350°F/regulo 4.

Sieve the dry ingredients (not the sugar) into a large, wide bowl. Rub in the butter. Now stir in the sugar.

Beat the eggs and whisk in the milk.

Mix the bread soda into the flour mixture. Beat with a wooden spoon until evenly combined. Stir in the walnuts.

Divide into the loaf tins and bake in the preheated oven for about 50–60 minutes or until a skewer comes out clean.

Leave to cool in the tins for about 5 minutes and then take out of the tins and leave to cool completely on a wire rack.

Introduction to
Sour Dough
Starters

So, you've caught the bread bug. You've worked your way through this book and now you're looking for a new challenge. Sour dough could be just what you have been waiting for. Be warned, though, once you commit yourself to making your own natural sour dough starter you will become passionate about its well-being. You will nurture it, feed it, and keep it safe, warm and out of draughts. Sounds a bit like having a baby in the house? Well, in many ways the sour dough starter *will* become your baby!

Over the years, I have been given jars of sour dough starter by other committed bread-makers. At first I would take good care of it, using it to make my own bread. But after a few weeks my interest would wane and I would forget to feed it. The starter would die and I would move on. I can say, hand on heart, I had no idea that when I first made my own starter it would come to mean so much to me. What I do know now is that if someone threw it out I would be devastated.

There are artisan bakers who have 30-year-old starters, and I have heard of families that have passed starters down through the generations. In some cases the starter is over 100 years old. Believe me, it's true!

Not only will you be finding somebody to mind your cat or dog when you go away on holiday but you will have to find a trusted friend to feed and care for your starter while you are gone.

'But what is this thing called a sour dough starter?' I hear you ask. Well, it is the ultimate way to create a loaf with superb texture and a complex flavour. It also improves the bread's keeping time and using a starter cuts out the need for a first rising in most of the breads you make.

What you are doing is creating for yourself a totally natural source of wild yeast. It takes about a week in the beginning before the yeast has time to thrive and grow. But, like they say, good things come to those who wait. You can't rush a natural starter.

A sour dough starter can be made with a number of ingredients, and there are so many ways you can encourage the yeast to feed and thrive. However, the basics are just flour and water. In this chapter, I have included, for example, a recipe for a potato starter. I have at times made a starter by putting a bunch of organic grapes into a muslin bag and soaking them in water for a day. I then use the grape water and the grapes still in their bag to make my starter. In place of the grapes you could use organic sultanas or raisins. The possibilities are endless.

When feeding your starter you can use all sorts of things. I sometimes pour in the cooled cooking water from potatoes. Or when I have a scrap of bread dough left over I put this into my starter too. It's amazing to see how it gets gobbled up over the next few days.

The first day you make the natural starter it will look unpromising. Cover it and keep it in a warm place. For the next two or three days it will begin to have little bubbles on the surface. Each day stir it, cover it again and keep it warm. On day 4 or 5 you may notice a marked difference. The mixture will have started to separate, a watery liquid will be on the top. Stir it well to combine it, cover it and set aside.

By day 6 or 7 your starter will be ready for its first outing. It should smell quite sour and fermented.

Once you have created your starter, taken care of it for that first week, you are then ready to take some of it out to make a sponge. Feed it with flour and leave it for 12–24 hours, it will become really active and excited.

The other starter you can make that does not require such a long-term commitment and produces a different taste is a sponge starter or biga. You will remember we used one in the ciabatta recipe. It is made from flour, water and a small amount of fresh yeast. It is usually left overnight to become active. You can use it then or store it in the fridge for 2–3 days. If you have not used the sponge by then throw it away and start again.

A bread made from a sponge starter like a bread made from a natural starter will keep for longer and have a more chewy and moist texture than a bread risen with yeast alone. Not all sour dough breads have to have a strong sour taste so don't be put off if you have tasted a sour dough loaf and found it

too sharp for your palette. There are many ways to reduce the powerful taste. I have a friend who was convinced that she did not really like sour dough, she found it far too acidic. Then I started to nurture my own starter and when she tasted my breads she was a convert to the cause!

Once your starter has matured and if you are not going to use it for a time it can be stored in the fridge for 2–3 weeks or you may also freeze it.

Until about 30 years ago most bakeries in Ireland would have always kept a little dough back each day and used it as a starter for the following mornings dough. A lot of artisan bakers still keep up this practice. When I baked a selection of breads each morning for the Garden Café I used to keep a lump of the previous day's yeast dough and use it the following morning. By doing this you are adding an already active piece of dough to your basic yeast bread, so it works in a similar way to a sponge starter. It improves the crust and the structure of the bread.

For some of the richer yeast breads like brioche, a sponge starter could be used to accelerate the yeast's activity. There are so many possibilities when using a starter. The amazing thing with any sour dough is that it is constantly changing and can be used to produce so many different results and effects.

There is another major advantage for rising breads using a natural sour dough. For reasons that are still unclear, there is an ever increasing growth in yeast allergies and yeast intolerance in today's society. So, for those of you out there who have candida or other yeast intolerance, this could be a way to enjoy yeast breads again without suffering.

In this chapter, I include recipes for natural starters and bigas and I cover the basic sour doughs that you can use them for. As your confidence in this area grows, so too will your sense of adventure. The more you use your starter, the more you will get a feel for what it can do.

First, though, some pointers for success with starters:

- Most important, **don't neglect it!**
- Use spring water and, where possible, water that is free of chlorine.
- Use organic flour.
- Keep the starter warm.
- Feed your starter.
- Every time you make a sponge, remember to feed the remaining starter in the bowl.
- The rising time depends on the activity of the yeast and the warmth of your kitchen.
- You can rise a natural dough in a cool place overnight so when you wake up in the morning you can have a loaf of bread out of the oven 45 minutes later for breakfast.

Basic Starter

This is a wild yeast starter and, would you believe, becomes active because of the yeast carried in the air. It takes 5–6 days before it is ready for use.

Makes: 1 starter, initially

What you need:
- 225 g/8 oz strong flour
- 225 ml/8 fl oz warm water
- 1 teaspoon sugar

What you do: In a plastic bowl, mix all the ingredients together. Cover with clingfilm and leave in a warm place for 24 hours.

Stir and cover tightly again.

Stir each day for 5–6 days. The mixture will become light and fluffy.

Potato Starter

This starter takes 5–6 days before it is ready for use.

Makes: 1 starter, initially

What you need:
- 200 ml/7 fl oz warm water
- 185 g/6$\frac{1}{2}$ oz flour
- 1 teaspoon sugar
- 1 medium potato, peeled and grated

What you do: In a plastic bowl, mix all the ingredients together. Cover with clingfilm and leave in a warm place for 24 hours.

Stir and cover tightly each day for 5–6 days.

The mixture will be light and fluffy when ready for use. It should smell quite sour and fermented.

Biga

Makes:	1 starter

What you need:
- 7 g/$\frac{1}{4}$ oz yeast
- 400 ml/14 fl oz warm water
- 500 g/1 lb 2 oz plain flour

What you do: Make the biga by stirring the yeast into 50 ml/2 fl oz warm water and leave until creamy, about 10 minutes. Stir in the remaining water and then the flour.

Put the biga into a lightly oiled bowl, cover with clingfilm and leave to rise at room temperature for 12–24 hours.

Brown Biga

Makes:	1 starter

What you need:
- 7 g/$\frac{1}{4}$ oz yeast
- 425 ml/15 fl oz warm water
- 110 g/4 oz strong white flour
- 310 g/11 oz wholemeal flour

What you do: As with the basic biga recipe, stir the yeast into 50 ml/2 fl oz warm water and leave until creamy, about 10 minutes. Stir in the remaining water and then the combined white and wholemeal flour.

Put the biga into a lightly oiled bowl, cover with clingfilm and let rise at room temperature for 12–24 hours.

White Sour Dough

The basic sour dough, loved for its chewy, tangy texture.

Makes:	2 loaves
Cooking time:	35–40 minutes

What you need:

Sponge:
- 250 g/9 oz starter of your choice
- 250 g/9 oz strong white flour
- 1 teaspoon sugar
- 170 ml/6 fl oz warm water

Dough:
- 150 ml/5 fl oz warm water
- 2 tablespoons olive oil
- 500 g/1 lb 2 oz strong white flour
- 1 teaspoon sugar
- 2 teaspoons salt
- 50 g/2 oz butter

What you do:

Fully preheat the oven to 230°C/450°F/regulo 8.

Mix the warm water into the starter in a large bowl. Stir well and add the flour and sugar. Cover and set aside for 12–24 hours for the sponge to become active.

The next day, make the dough by putting the sponge in the bowl of an electric mixer. Add in the warm water and olive oil and blend for approximately 1 minute.

Beat in the flour, butter, sugar and salt. Mix to form a very soft, light and pliable dough.

Turn the dough out onto a lightly floured work surface and knead for a few minutes.

Split the ball of dough and shape into 2 free-form loaves on a well-oiled baking sheet. The dough will be quite soft. Cover with a clean tea-towel. Leave to rise for 5–6 hours or overnight in a cool place.

Bake for 35–40 minutes. When you think it is cooked, tap it and listen for the hollow sound. Allow to cool on a wire rack.

Brown Sour Dough

This easy, chewy sour dough is so delicious, it can be quite addictive!

Makes:	2 loaves
Cooking time:	35–40 minutes

What you need: **Sponge:**
- 250 g/9 oz starter of your choice
- 250 g/9 oz strong white flour
- 1 teaspoon sugar
- 170 ml/6 fl oz warm water

Dough:
- 425 ml/15 fl oz warm water
- 400 g/14 oz brown flour
- 50 g/2 oz strong white flour
- 1 teaspoon treacle
- 2 teaspoons salt

- 2 loaf tins, well-oiled

What you do: Preheat the oven to 230°C/450°F/regulo 8.

In a large bowl, mix the warm water into the starter. Stir well and add the flour and sugar. Cover and set aside for 12–24 hours for the sponge to become active.

The next day, make the dough. Put the sponge in the bowl of an electric mixer, add the warm water and treacle, blend for approximately 1 minute.

Add the flours and salt. Mix to form a loose dough, too wet to knead.

Halve the dough and place in the loaf tins, covering each with a clean tea-towel. Leave to rise until doubled in size, which will take about 5–6 hours, depending on the warmth of your kitchen and the moisture in the air. Or, alternatively, leave to rise in a cool place overnight.

Place in your oven for 35–40 minutes. Remove the bread from the tin about 10 minutes before the end of cooking and put it back in the oven to crisp all round. Check the bread is fully cooked by listening for the hollow sound when you tap it. Allow to cool on a wire rack.

Malted Sour Dough

A super malted loaf with the hint of fennel, one of the ultimate flavour combinations.

Makes:	2 loaves
Cooking time:	35–40 minutes

What you need:

Sponge:
- 125 ml/4 fl oz starter of your choice
- 225 g/8 oz strong white flour
- 1 teaspoon sugar
- 225 ml/8 fl oz warm water

Dough:
- 450 g/1 lb granary flour and
- 110 g/4 oz strong white flour
- 2 teaspoons salt
- 50 g/2 oz butter
- 1 teaspoon treacle
- 2 tablespoon olive oil
- 225 ml/8 fl oz warm water
- 2–3 tablespoons fennel seeds

- 2 loaf tins, well-oiled

What you do:

Fully preheat your oven to 230°C/450°F/regulo 8.

In a large bowl, mix the warm water into the starter. Stir well and add the flour and sugar. Cover and set aside for 12–24 hours for the sponge to become active.

Next day, make the dough by putting the sponge in the bowl of an electric mixer and adding the warm water and olive oil. Blend for about 1 minute.

Beat in the flour, butter and salt. Mix to form a very soft, light and pliable dough.

Turn out onto a lightly floured work surface and knead for a few minutes.

Scatter the base of the oiled loaf tins with fennel seeds, keeping back enough to sprinkle on top of the risen loaves.

Divide the dough into the loaf tins, cover them both with a clean tea-towel. Leave to rise for 5–6 hours depending on the warmth of your kitchen and the moisture in the air. The dough will rise well above the rim.

Brush lightly with water and sprinkle with the remaining fennel seeds.

Place in your oven for 35–40 minutes. Remove the bread from the tin about 10 minutes before the end of cooking and put it back into the oven to crisp it up nicely. Tap the bread as usual to test when it is fully cooked. Cool on a wire rack.

Rye Sour Dough

My version of a New York rye sour dough. Great eaten with smoked meats.

Makes: 2 loaves

Cooking time: 35–40 minutes

What you need: **Sponge:**
- 120 ml/4 fl oz starter of your choice
- 170 g/6 oz strong white flour
- 50 g/2 oz dark rye flour
- 1 teaspoon sugar
- 225 ml/8 fl oz warm water

Dough:
- 275 ml/10 fl oz warm water
- 340 g/12 oz strong white flour
- 140 g/5 oz dark rye flour
- 25 g/1 oz caraway seeds
- 1 teaspoon salt
- 50 g/2 oz butter

- 2 loaf tins, well-oiled

What you do: Preheat the oven to 230°C/450°F/regulo 8.

In a large bowl, mix the water into the starter. Stir well and add the flours and sugar. Cover and set aside for 12–24 hours for the sponge to become active.

The following day, make the dough by putting the sponge in the bowl of an electric mixer. Add the warm water and blend for approximately 1 minute.

Beat in the flour, butter, caraway seeds and salt. Mix to form a very soft, light and pliable dough.

Turn the dough out onto a lightly floured work surface and knead for a few minutes. Then divide into 2 halves and put the dough into the well-oiled loaf tins, cover them each with a clean tea-towel. Leave to rise for 5–6 hours, until the dough is well above the rim.

Place in your preheated oven for 35–40 minutes. Remove the bread from the tin about 10 minutes before the end of cooking and put it back into the oven to crisp all round. Cool on a wire rack.

Honeycombed Sour Dough

This soft honeycombed loaf is baked after the first rising. The wetness of the dough gives a wonderful chewy textured loaf. I discovered it quite by accident but it is now a firm favourite. The flavour will depend on how long your dough is rising.

Makes: 2 loaves

Cooking time: 30–35 minutes

What you need:
- 450 g/1 lb biga
- 250 g/9 oz flour
- 2 teaspoons salt
- 7 g/$\frac{1}{2}$oz fresh yeast
- 50ml/2 fl oz warm milk
- 150 ml/5 fl oz warm water
- 1 dessertspoon olive oil

What you do: Preheat the oven to 220°C/425°F/regulo 7.

Stir the yeast into the warm milk in the bowl of an electric mixer, let stand for about 10 minutes. Add the water, oil and biga.

Mix with the paddle until blended. Add the flour and salt, mix for 10 minutes. Change to the dough hook and beat for 15–25 minutes at high speed, or until the dough is stringy and pulling away from the sides of the bowl. Getting the dough to this stage is essential.

Divide the dough between two oiled bread tins. Leave to rise in a warm place for 1–1$\frac{1}{2}$ hours or until dough has doubled in size and is peeping out over the top of the tins.

Dust lightly with flour before baking. Bake for 30–35 minutes. Cool on wire racks.

Introduction to
Bread as the Base

The expression, 'the bread of life', had to begin somewhere, in some folk memory or tradition. So, in honour of this, my aim in this chapter is to introduce to you a handful of special recipes that use 'bread as the base'.

Bread is so very versatile. It can truly be a meal in itself. The humble sandwich, for example, the toasted sandwich, a Mexican quesadilla or tortilla wrap, pitta bread filled with spicy chicken. That's just the beginning. Ultimately, there are, of course, so many recipes that use bread as the base that I have only been able to include a few here.

But the key is your imagination. In Grandpa's Bramley Bread, for example, I use apples, but you could replace them with rhubarb or gooseberries, or you could mix blackcurrants or blackberries with the apples. In the Shannon Chicken Casserole, you could use lamb or pork instead. Bread is the common element in an endless list of delicious creations. There are no limits with bread as the base.

Bread is truly the foundation, the starting point for countless gastronomical delights.

Brown Bread Ice Cream

For years I have had my doubts about this ice cream until I started to caramelise the brown breadcrumbs. I always use brown soda bread as I think it gives the best texture. The end result is a crunchy nutty effect through the ice cream. It is a quick way to smarten up a good quality shop-bought vanilla ice cream, or a tasty way to enjoy your home-made ice cream even more than usual.

Makes: 450 g/1 lb

Cooking time: 5 minutes, approximately

What you need:
- 110 g/4 oz brown soda bread (see page 7), finely crumbed
- 110 g/4 oz sugar
- home-made ice cream (see page 147 for Ballymaloe Vanilla Ice Cream)
- 1 loaf tin, lined with clingfilm

What you do: In a heavy-based frying pan, mix the brown breadcrumbs and the sugar. Heat on a high temperature for about 5 minutes. Resist the urge to stir it too much. Lift and tilt the pan to move the crumb and sugar mixture if it starts to colour unevenly.

It needs to be golden throughout. When it has all caramelised, turn it out onto a sheet of baking parchment and allow to cool.

When cooled, put into a transparent plastic bag and crush roughly with a rolling pin.

In a bowl, beat the ice cream and fold in the caramelised crumb. Scrape into the lined loaf tin and freeze until required.

Take out of the freezer 20 minutes before serving. Sprinke with a little extra caramelised crumb.

French Toast

A breakfast classic, speedy and easy to do. In and out of the pan in about just a few minutes.
I serve it with castor sugar but you can also eat it with maple syrup or with a fried breakfast.

Makes:	6–8 slices
Cooking time:	5 minutes, approximately
What you need:	• 2 eggs
	• 4 tablespoons cream
	• 15 g/$\frac{1}{2}$ oz butter
	• 6–8 slices white soda bread or white yeast bread (see pages 2 and 38 respectively)
	• castor sugar to taste
	• heavy-based frying pan
What you do:	In a Pyrex bowl, whisk the eggs and cream. Pour into a shallow, wide bowl.
	Heat the frying pan on a medium heat and melt the butter.
	Dip the slices of bread into the egg mixture and coat completely. Fry 2 slices of the bread in the pan until just golden on each side.
	Serve hot and sprinkled with castor sugar.

Ivan Allen's Bramley Bread

The sweet bread topping in this recipe makes a great contrast to the apples underneath.
Try a little grated ginger in place of the cinnamon for an extra zing.

Makes:	8–10 servings
Cooking time:	45 minutes, approximately

What you need:
- 900 g/2 lb bramley apples
- 85 g/3 oz granulated sugar
- 1 teaspoon ground cinnamon

Topping:
- 225 g/8 oz flour
- 50 g/2 oz castor sugar
- 1 teaspoon baking powder
- pinch of salt
- 110 g/4 oz butter
- 2 eggs
- 175 ml/6 fl oz milk
- egg wash
- granulated sugar

- ceramic baking dish

What you do:
Preheat the oven to 180°C/350°F/regulo 4.

Peel, core and chop the apples roughly. Place in the base of the baking dish, sprinkle with the sugar and cinnamon.

Sieve all the dry ingredients into a bowl. Cut the butter into cubes and rub into the flour until the mixture resembles coarse breadcrumbs.

Whisk the egg with the milk. Make a well in the centre of the dry ingredients, pour in the liquid all at once and mix to a soft dough.

Turn out onto a well-floured work surface and shape to fit your dish. Gently lift the dough and position over the apples.

Brush the top with egg wash and sprinkle with sugar.

Bake in the fully preheated oven for 45 minutes or until the top is crusty and golden and the apples soft and juicy.

Remove from the oven and set aside for a few minutes.

Serve warm with soft brown sugar and cream or, if you prefer, ice cream (see page 147 for my home-made ice cream recipe).

Shannon Chicken Casserole with Herb Scones

This chicken casserole is another one of my stand-by dishes. I first began to make it when on holiday with my children in a boat on the Shannon. It is perfect for many occasions but it was ideal for the boating holidays as I had just one oven, which is unusual for me! With this dish I cooked the main meal and the bread all in one pot. So, when the children came in cold and hungry after a day of frolicking and fun, this soon had them comforted and happy. And once back home there were frequent demands for 'Daddy's Shannon dinner'.

Makes: 4–6 servings

Cooking time: 1 hour–1 hour 10 minutes

What you need:
- 1 chicken, 1.57 kg/3$\frac{1}{2}$ lb, preferably free-range
- a little butter or oil for sautéing
- 170 g/6 oz green streaky bacon
- 340 g/12 oz carrot, peeled and cut into chunks
- 450 g/1 lb onions, baby onions are nicest
- sprig of thyme
- 700 ml/1$\frac{1}{4}$ pints home-made chicken stock
- roux, optional (see page 146)
- 1 tablespoon parsley, freshly chopped
- soda bread with herbs, half quantities (see recipe page 3)
- egg wash
- grated cheddar cheese

What you do: Preheat the oven to 180°C/350°F/regulo 4.

Cut the rind off the bacon and cut the bacon into approximately 1 cm/$\frac{1}{2}$ in cubes. Divide the chicken into 8 chunky joints. Season well with salt and freshly ground pepper.

Heat a little oil in a heavy-based frying pan and cook the bacon until crisp, remove and transfer to the casserole.

Add the chicken pieces a few at a time to the pan and sauté until golden. Transfer to the bacon in the casserole and season well with salt and freshly ground pepper.

Heat control is crucial here. The pan mustn't burn, yet it must be hot enough to brown the chicken. If it is too cool, the chicken pieces will stew rather than sauté and as a result the meat may be tough.

Then toss the onion and carrot in the pan, adding a little butter if necessary. Add to the casserole.

Degrease the pan and deglaze with stock, bring to the boil and pour over the chicken. Season well, add the sprig of thyme and bring to simmering point on top of the stove, then put into the hot oven for 30–40 minutes.

When the chicken is just cooked, strain off the cooking liquid, degrease, return the degreased liquid to the casserole and bring to the boil.

Turn up the oven temperature to 230°C/450°F/regulo 8.

Thicken with a little roux at this stage.

Add the meat, carrots and onions back into the casserole and bring to the boil. Taste and correct the seasoning.

Roll out the soda bread dough into a round, 2 cm/$\frac{1}{2}$ in thick, stamp out circles with a 5 cm/2 in cutter.

Cover the top of the stew with slightly overlapping herb scones, brush with egg wash and sprinkle with a little cheese if you wish.

Bake in the hot oven for 8–10 minutes, then reduce the heat to 200°C/400°F/regulo 6 for a further 20 minutes or until the crust is baked.

Introduction to
Essential Extras

In this chapter, you will find a treasure trove of recipes that are not breads themselves but which go well with, or play some important part in, the recipes featured in this book. Indeed, they are specifically mentioned at various points throughout the book.

I feel very strongly that you can't beat home-made jams. Anyone who knows me or who has seen me demonstrate will know that I believe there is no point in going to the trouble of making something as luxurious as brioches or croissants if you don't make your own jam to go with them.

And I have included two recipes for tomato sauce to serve with pizzas. One is oven roasted and the other sauce is cooked on the hob.

I hope you will enjoy these essential extras and use them regularly in your own repertoire to impress and delight your family and friends.

A Buttermilk Plant

Every year at the school we proudly teach hundreds of students from all over the world how to make Irish soda breads, which soon become addictive.

It can sometimes be difficult to source buttermilk commercially so here is a recipe for a buttermilk plant. It will increase and multiply and after a few weeks you will be in a position to pass some on to your friends.

Makes:	1 plant, initially
What you need:	• 25 g/1 oz sugar • 25 g/1 oz yeast • 600 ml/1 pint tepid milk • 600 ml/1 pint tepid water
What you do:	In a clean bowl, cream the yeast with the sugar, then gradually add the tepid milk and water combined.

Transfer the mixture into a bowl that can easily be washed and scalded.

Cover the bowl with clingfilm and leave it in a warm place for a couple of days. The milk will smell and taste like buttermilk when it is ready to use.

Put a piece of muslin in the bottom of a sieve and strain the milk through this. The liquid that pours through the sieve is your very own home-produced buttermilk.

The funny-looking thing like lumpy cornflour which remains in the sieve will be the plant. Rinse every drop of milk off it by pouring a cup of tepid water over it. Let the water run through the strainer into the buttermilk.

To start a new lot of buttermilk, scrape the plant off the muslin and put it back into the scalded and well-rinsed bowl. Add another 2 pints of tepid milk and water, cover it and leave it as before to increase and multiply.

That first ounce of yeast will go on growing and multiplying, giving you buttermilk until the end of time. But the plant needs a certain amount of care:

- It must be strained at least every five days. If you don't want the milk for baking, you can always drink it.
- Make sure the milk and water is never more than luke warm. Strong heat kills yeast.
- Cleanliness is very important. The careful rinsing after straining and the scalding of the container are both essential if the plant is to live.

Raspberry Jam

Of all the jams, raspberry jam is the easiest and quickest to make. I'm sure it's everyone's favourite. Eat it with Penny's Perthshire Butteries (see page 102), fresh scones or a host of other breads.

Makes:	3–4 pots of jam
Cooking time:	15 minutes, approximately
What you need:	• 900 g/2 lb fresh raspberries
	• 900 g/2 lb white sugar
	• 4 jam jars, 450 g/1 lb each
What you do:	Preheat the oven to 180°C/350°F/regulo 4.

Wash, dry and sterilise the jars in the preheated oven, for 15 minutes.

Heat the sugar in the oven for 5–10 minutes. Chill a plate in the fridge.

Put the raspberries into a wide, stainless-steel saucepan and cook for 3–4 minutes until the juice begins to run.

Add the hot sugar and stir over a gentle heat until the sugar is fully dissolved. Increase the heat and boil steadily for about 5 minutes, stirring frequently.

Test for a set by putting about a teaspoon of jam on the cold plate and leaving it for a few minutes in a cool place. It should then wrinkle when pushed with a finger.

Remove the jam from the heat immediately. Skim and pour into the jam jars. Cover straight away while the jam is still hot.

Hide the jam in a cool place or store it on a shelf in your kitchen so you can feel great every time you look at it! Wherever you put it, it will be so delicious, it won't be there long!

Strawberry Jam

Home-made strawberry jam can be truly sensational, but the fruit must be of a high quality. If you follow this recipe carefully you will have no problems. However, it is often thought to be one of the most difficult jams to set because strawberries are low in pectin, so don't attempt it if your fruit is not perfect.

Once you have made it successfully though, you'll find you can't have brioche without your home-made strawberry jam.

Makes: 7–8 pots

Cooking time: 15 minutes, approximately

What you need:
- 1.8 kg/4 lb unblemished strawberries
- 1.8 kg/4 lb granulated sugar
- 2 lemons, squeezed

- 8 jam jars, 450 g/1 lb each

What you do: Preheat the oven to 180°C/350°F/regulo 4.

Wash, dry and sterilise the jars in the preheated oven, for 15 minutes.

Heat the sugar in the oven for 5–10 minutes. Chill a plate in the fridge.

Put the strawberries into a wide, stainless-steel saucepan, with the lemon juice.

Use a potato masher to crush about three-quarters or more of the berries.

Bring to the boil and cook the strawberries in the juice for 2–3 minutes.

Add the warmed sugar to the fruit. Stir over a gentle heat until the sugar is dissolved. Then boil for about 10–15 minutes, stirring frequently. Strawberry jam sticks and burns very easily, so be careful.

Test for a set by putting about a teaspoon of jam on the cold plate and leaving it in a cool place. After a few minutes, it should wrinkle when pushed with a finger.

Remove the jam from the heat immediately you have reached the setting point. Skim and pour the jam into the sterilised jam jars. Cover straight away while the jam is still hot.

Store in a cool, dry cupboard.

Chocolate Butter

We serve this yummy butter with chocolate buns (see page 85) and also with our vanilla bread. You will no doubt find your own favourite bread and chocolate butter combination.

Makes:	8–10 generous servings
What you need:	• 110 g/4 oz unsalted butter, melted • 25 g/1 oz unsweetened chocolate • pinch of salt • 2 teaspoons vanilla extract • 140 g/5 oz icing sugar
What you do:	Half-fill a saucepan with water and bring it to the boil, put the chocolate and butter into a Pyrex bowl and place this over the pan of water, making sure the base of the bowl does not touch the water. Turn off the heat under the saucepan. Leave the chocolate and butter to melt in the bowl. Add the sugar, salt and vanilla to the chocolate mixture and beat until smooth and well blended. Transfer to a butter dish or pretty bowl. Serve the butter at room temperature but store it in the fridge.

Marzipan

This marzipan is used not only in the Stollen recipe on page 61 but has a host of other uses.

Makes:	450 g/1 lb
What you need:	• 170 g/6 oz ground almonds • 225 g/8 oz sugar • 63 ml/2$\frac{1}{2}$ fl oz water • 1 egg white • 1 drop natural almond essence

What you do: In a heavy-based saucepan, dissolve the sugar in the water and bring it to the boil. Cook to 116°C/240°F or to the 'soft ball' stage, keeping the sides of the saucepan brushed down with water.

Remove from the heat and stir the syrup until cloudy. Add the ground almonds, essence and slightly beaten egg whites. Mix very well. Turn into a bowl and allow it to become cool and firm.

Home-made marzipan will keep for 3–4 weeks in a fridge.

Kinoith Summer Garden Salad with Timmy's Dressing

A green salad, the perfect accompaniment to almost any meal. When I make this salad, glistening with my honey dressing, I can never seem to make enough. The dressing must be made freshly so resist the temptation to make a huge quantity and store it in the fridge. The other important thing to note is that this dressing must not be made in a blender.

Makes: 4 servings

What you need: **Timmy's Dressing:**
- 3 tablespoons olive oil
- 1 tablespoon white wine vinegar
- salt and freshly ground pepper to taste
- 1 teaspoon honey
- 1 heaped teaspoon wholegrain honey mustard
- 2 cloves garlic, crushed

Salad:
- a selection of fresh lettuce and salad leaves
- herbs of your choice
- edible flowers, if available

What you do: First, make the dressing in a bowl. Mix all the ingredients together and whisk well till completely blended. Taste the dressing. It should be slightly sweet. If it is too bitter, a bit more honey.

Wash and dry the lettuce and salad leaves. If large, tear into bite-sized bits. Put them all into a deep salad bowl, add the herbs and edible flowers.

Just before serving toss the salad in just enough dressing to make the leaves glisten.

Isaac's Roasted Tomato Sauce

This is a tomato sauce my son Isaac developed for a pizza topping. It is best made in the summer when the tomatoes are really ripe.

Cooking time:	15–20 minutes
What you need:	• 450 g/1 lb very ripe tomatoes, halved • 6 cloves of garlic, unpeeled • 1 tablespoon balsamic vinegar • 2 tablespoons olive oil • salt, pepper, sugar to taste
What you do:	Preheat the oven to 220°C/425°F/regulo 7.

Put the tomatoes and garlic on a roasting tray, in a single layer, seeds facing up. Season the tomatoes with salt, pepper and sugar. Sprinkle with the vinegar and oil.

Roast in your nice hot oven for 15–20 minutes until the tomatoes are completely soft and the garlic is squishy.

Blend all the ingredients to a smooth paste, push through a sieve to remove all the skins and seeds. Taste and correct seasoning.

Garlic Butter

Makes:	110 g/4 oz, approximately
What you need:	• 110 g/4 oz butter • 2 tablespoons parsley, finely chopped • 4–5 teaspoons lemon juice, freshly squeezed • 4–5 cloves garlic, crushed
What you do:	Cream the butter. Stir in the lemon juice a few drops of at a time, then add the parsley and the crushed garlic. Mix well.

To store, form into a roll and wrap in greaseproof paper, screwing each end tight so that it looks like a cracker.

Piperonata

Makes: 8–10 servings

Cooking time: 30 minutes, approximately

What you need:
- 1 onion, sliced
- 1 clove of garlic, crushed
- 2 red peppers
- 2 green peppers
- 6 large tomatoes, dark red and very ripe
- 2 tablespoons olive oil
- salt
- pepper, freshly ground
- pinch of sugar
- a few leaves of fresh basil, if available

What you do: Into a heavy-bottomed saucepan over a gentle heat, place the oil, onions and garlic, cover with a butter wrapper and lid. Leave to soften while the peppers and tomatoes are being prepared.

Halve the peppers, remove the seeds carefully, cut into quarters and then into strips across rather than lengthways.

Add to the pan and stir in lightly, replace the lid and continue to cook on a low heat.

Peel the tomatoes by scalding in boiling water for 10 seconds, then pour off the water. Remove the skins immediately. Slice the peeled tomatoes and add to the pan, season with salt, freshly ground pepper, sugar and the few leaves of fresh basil. Cook until the vegetables are just soft, about 30 minutes.

Apart from the middle of the summer when tomatoes are very ripe, it is often best to use tinned whole tomatoes to get a really good flavour.

Timmy's Tomato Fondue

My constant companion and fallback in the kitchen is a tomato fondue. Earlier in this book, I used it as a pizza topping but I also serve it at home with roast chicken or any roast meat. Tomato fondue makes a great sauce for pasta. No matter how bare your kitchen cupboard is, you are bound to have onions, garlic and a tin of tomatoes, so I believe this may become one of your permanent stand-by recipes too!

Makes: 4–6 servings

Cooking time: 20–30 minutes

What you need:
- 110 g/4 oz sliced onions
- 1 clove of garlic, crushed
- 1 dessertspoon olive oil
- 450 g/1 lb very ripe tomatoes, use tinned in winter
- salt and freshly ground pepper to taste
- pinch of sugar
- 2–3 tablespoons parsley and/or annual marjoram, chopped

What you do: In a heavy-based saucepan, sweat the sliced onions and garlic in oil on a gentle heat for about 10 minutes, until soft but not browned.

It is vital for the success of this dish that the onions are completely soft before the tomatoes are added.

To skin the tomatoes, put them into a deep bowl and cover them with boiling water. Count 10 seconds and then pour off the water immediately; peel off the skins and slice the tomatoes.

Add the tomatoes to the onions. Season with salt, freshly ground pepper and sugar and add a generous sprinkling of your choice of chopped herbs.

Cook for 10–20 minutes more, or until the tomato softens. Add lots of chopped fresh herbs just before serving.

Roux

Makes: 225 g/8 oz

Cooking time: 2–3 minutes

What you need:
- 110 g/4 oz butter
- 110 g/4 oz flour

What you do: Melt the butter and cook the flour in it for 2 minutes on a low heat, stirring occasionally. Use as required. It will keep for at least a fortnight in a refrigerator.

Ballymaloe Vanilla Ice Cream

This Ballymaloe Ice Cream is very rich and very delicious, made on an egg mousse base with softly whipped cream and flavourings added. Ice creams made in this way have a smooth texture and do not need further whisking during the freezing period. They should not be served frozen hard.

Makes: 6–8 servings

What you need:
- 50 g/2 oz sugar
- 120 ml/4 fl oz water
- 2 egg yolks
- $\frac{1}{2}$ teaspoon pure vanilla essence
- 600 ml/1 pint softly whipped cream

What you do: Put the egg yolks into a bowl and whisk until light and fluffy.

Combine the sugar and water in a small heavy-bottomed saucepan, stir over heat until the sugar is completely dissolved, then remove the spoon and boil the syrup until it reaches the 'thread' stage, 106–113°C/200–220°F. It will look thick and syrupy; when a metal spoon is dipped in, the last drops of syrup will form thin threads.

Pour this boiling syrup in a steady stream onto the egg yolks, whisking all the time.

Add the vanilla essence and continue to whisk until it becomes a thick, creamy, white mousse.

Fold the softly whipped cream into the mousse, pour into a bowl, cover and freeze.

Remove from the freezer at least 10 minutes before serving.

Glossary

Baker's flour. An alternative name for strong flour or bread flour. It has a higher gluten content, being milled from hard wheat.

Biga. The Italian word for a sponge starter. Made with flour, water and a little yeast, it is often added to ciabatta and used to leaven this classical Italian bread. It gives the bread a light, chewy consistency. See also **Sponge** and **Starter**.

Bowls. A selection of bowls is useful in any kitchen. For soda bread I sometimes use a large, plastic, washing-up bowl. Ceramic bowls are best for rising.

Bread soda. Also know as bicarbonate of soda or baking soda. Always measure bread soda very carefully and sieve finely as lumps of bread soda do not dissolve readily.

Butter. Always use pure butter, *never* substitute with margarine.

Buttermilk. Easily available commercially in most countries. It may vary in consistency, so if it is very thin you will not need as much. See also the recipe for a Buttermilk Plant on page 139.

Cooking times. Cooking times will vary from oven to oven. Get to know your oven and its temperatures and idiosyncrasies.

Deglazing. A simple technique to capture all the juices and flavours from a stew or pan-cooked dish. First, remove the meat and vegetables from the casserole and then pour off any surplus fat from the liquid. Bring the liquid to a high heat, thus reducing the liquid and intensifying the flavours. Scrape any delicious sediment from the base of the pan. Return the meat and vegetables.

Dried yeast. A concentrated form of yeast, use only half fresh yeast quantities. Otherwise, use as you would fresh yeast. See also **Fast-acting yeast** and **Yeast**.

Egg wash. A mixture of egg and usually a little cream or milk.

Eggs. Use free-range eggs wherever possible.

Electric mixer. If you plan on making a lot of bread, investing in an electric mixer is worthwhile. A heavy-duty mixer like a Kenwood or a kitchen aid is ideal.

Fast-acting yeast. You will normally buy this in sachets. Follow the directions on the back of the packet. It is usually added straight into the flour. See also **Dried yeast** and **Yeast**.

Flour. Where possible, use organic flour.

Gluten. Enables the bread to rise by capturing the carbon dioxide from the yeast and trapping it in the dough.

Granary flour. A mixture of wholemeal, white and rye flour with some malted grains. Improves keeping time of bread.

Herbs. Only use fresh herbs if you can.

Kibbled wheat. Wheat of which the kernel has been gently cracked.

Kneading. Pushing, stretching and folding the dough so as to activate and develop the gluten in the flour.

Knocking back. Pushing the air out of the dough after the first rising.

Ovens. Get to know your oven and its temperatures and idiosyncrasies. Most breads cook best in a conventional oven.

Pepper. Use freshly ground black pepper.

Plain flour. A multi-purpose flour produced from a blend of soft and hard wheat.

Rising times. The time it takes a bread to rise depends on the warmth of the kitchen and the moisture in the atmosphere, and in the dough. The warmer and more humid an atmosphere, the quicker will be the rising time. However, the best results are usually gained from not rising the dough too quickly.

Salt. Essential in bread-making. Use good quality pure rock salt, or where indicated, as in some bread recipes, sea salt.

Semolina. Flour milled from durum wheat.

Spices. Whenever possible, use freshly ground spices.

Sponge. A starter made from flour, water and a tiny amount of yeast. It is allowed to ferment, often overnight and is then mixed into a bread dough. See also **Biga** and **Starter**.

Starter. A natural sour dough starter, essentially made from a mixture of flour and water. It is left to ferment and develop to maturity over a period of about a week before use. It bubbles, rises and ferments, often tripling in volume. A portion of this starter is then used to leaven dough. The rest of the starter is fed and, with care, can be maintained over extremely long periods of time. See also **Biga** and **Sponge**.

Strong flour. Sometimes called baker's flour or bread flour. It has a higher gluten content, being milled from hard wheat.

Warm water. By 'warm' I mean 'blood heat', that is, 37°C/97°F.

Wholemeal flour. Sometimes called whole wheat pastry flour, it is made from the whole wheat kernel.

Yeast. When I refer to yeast in this book, unless stated otherwise, I mean fresh yeast. It can be stored in the fridge, tightly covered for up to 3 weeks, or it can be frozen. Fresh yeast can be bought from baker's and from the bakery department of most supermarkets. See also **Dried yeast** and **Fast-acting yeast**.

Zest. The outer layer of the skin on a citrus fruit. Usually grated and used as a flavouring.

Index